WITHDRAWN

USING STRUCTURED DESIGN

Using Structured Design

How To Make Programs Simple,
Changeable, Flexible, and Reusable

WAYNE P. STEVENS

A WILEY-INTERSCIENCE PUBLICATION

JOHN WILEY & SONS, New York • Chichester • Brisbane • Toronto • Singapore

Library of Congress Cataloging in Publication Data:

Stevens, Wayne P.   1944-
   Using structured design.

   "A Wiley-Interscience publication."
   Bibliography: p.
   Includes index.
   1. Structured programming.   I.   Title.

QA76.6.S74   001.64'2   80-23481
ISBN 0-471-08198-1

To my wife, Penny
"There will never be another you"

Foreword

The hope of every pioneer is that others will use the pathways newly opened, that later explorers will open up still further territories, and that someday what was once a narrow trail will become a well-traveled highway. As one of the pathfinders of the "structural revolution" in computer programming, it is satisfying now to be able to survey the new regions of "structured programming," "structured design," and "structured analysis," and find them rich in resources, abundant with proven applications. The route had already been well marked through years of careful survey and construction, when, in 1974, Wayne Stevens, a consummate politician, assembled the unlikely team that would publish the now classic paper, "Structured Design." Second author Glen Myers was the first to put theory and technique into book form with *Composite Design*. It took Ed Yourdon's coauthorship with me to produce the ambitious and long-awaited *Structured Design: Fundamentals of a Discipline of Computer Program and System Design* (Prentice-Hall, 1979). And now, an era of pioneering seems to be nearing its close, as the third of those three original authors produces his book, a book emphasizing—fittingly, I think—*application* of the principles and techniques of structured design.

The working programmer, the program designer, and the systems analyst will find in this book a singularly practical guide to building systems that take less time to put together, take apart, and put together again. We can at last say this with something more than the confidence of dreamers, for structured design has proven itself in demanding trials ranging from procedures of only a few hundred steps written for a programmable calculator to a design support system consisting of hundreds of thousands of lines of COBOL.

This book fulfills its promise of making the powerful tools of structured design more accessible. It provides not a shortcut, but a well-marked thruway for the first-time traveler. Theory here may sometimes be bypassed temporarily, or streamlined, but it is never seriously slighted. Stevens has collected numerous examples illustrating the effective application of structured design. Particularly useful is his original compilation in Chapter 7 of guidelines and techniques for improving program structure. There are more here than I would have thought existed, each one clearly presented and realistically illustrated.

All the examples, from brief descriptions of local decisions to complete program designs, are well worked out in sufficient detail to be meaningful and convincing to even the neophyte designer. Clarity is not achieved by oversimplifying, and a healthy respect is maintained for those aspects of design that remain matters of judgment and creative compromise. The designer is given well-built tools, not a cookbook.

Imitation may be flattering, but the real wish of every teacher is to be exceeded by former students. Wayne Stevens does not merely rehash what has been covered before, but adds a genuine contribution to the growing literature of this field, a contribution that belongs on the desk of every serious programming professional and in the library of every organization interested in reducing the spiraling costs of program development and maintenance.

LARRY L. CONSTANTINE

Preface

Structured design is a program design technique that reduces the effort necessary to implement and maintain programs. With structured design it takes less time to produce more changeable, flexible, and reusable code than it takes to write a monolithic program. Structured design suggests dividing programs into single-function, separately compiled modules. Advantages are gained because a one-page module is easier to write than one page of a larger program. Structured designed programs are simpler, so they tend to run as fast or faster than monolithic programs.

Structured design can also be used to design macros, catalogued procedures, machine instructions, and functions to be microcoded. It can be used to break down the complexity of large systems during systems analysis and diesgn phases, and to choose the functions to be made available at nodes in a distributed processing system. In general, structured design is useful whenever it is desirable to divide larger functions into relatively independent pieces.

Readers who will be using structured design and are unfamiliar with its concepts and techniques will probably find it worthwhile to read the entire book in the order presented. Those who are somewhat familiar with structured design can probably identify by title the chapters that are of interest. Chapter summaries include the basic subjects discussed and recommendations made in the chapter. A review of the summary for any chapter can help identify whether or not the chapter includes areas of interest.

A conceptual overview of structured design can be gained by reading the chapter summaries and skipping Chapters 7, 9, and 10. Chapters 1, 2, and 13 are highly recommended for all readers.

WAYNE STEVENS

Fairfield, Connecticut
October 1980

Acknowledgments

Much of the material included in this book was previously published in the *IBM Systems Journal* in a somewhat different form. Their permission to include it here in its updated form is appreciated.

Figures 4.14, 6.4, 6.11, 6.12, and 7.4 were adapted from Edward Yourdan, Larry L. Constantine, *Structured Design; Fundamentals of a Discipline of Computer Program and Systems Design*, © 1979, by permission of Prentice Hall, Inc., Englewood Cliffs, New Jersey.

My thanks to Keith Warltier for inviting me to present a course in structured design. It was that course which started my work in developing this approach in how to do structured design to augment what was published in the *IBM Systems Journal*. Thanks also for the substantial work George Hathaway and Capers Jones did reviewing the manuscript and for their suggestions for improving it. And a special thanks goes to my family for putting up with all the time I took out to do this book.

Most of all, though, thanks should go to Larry Constantine. It was his forward thinking in the early 1960s that led to the birth of structured design. He provided a firm foundation on which others could build and extend the concepts he discovered. Best wishes in your new career, Larry, and thanks.

W.S.

Contents

1
About This Book

The primary purpose of this book is to enhance the reader's ability to make use of the concepts of structured design. It is aimed primarily at those who are responsible for developing programs. The programs to be developed may be application programs for use within the company, programs which are to be sold, operating systems, support programs, and programs that are being rewritten either completely or partially. Structured design can also be applied directly to the development of macros, cataloged procedures or EXECS, subroutine libraries, utility modules, and functions to be microcoded. It is useful wherever low development cost, ease of maintenance, flexibility, and ease of use are important. It can also be used to reduce the effort needed to produce code that must run quickly or make low use of real memory. This is possible because structured designed programs can be efficiently, rapidly, and accurately optimized.

This book is intended for both experienced and beginning programmers and analysts. Throughout the book, alternatives are examined in the light of structured design concepts. Experienced readers may find some of the alternatives familiar. But whether or not the reader is familiar with the problems, the discussion of the alternatives serves to illustrate the concepts being explained.

A basic understanding of programming concepts is assumed. Examples of code, where they are necessary, are given in relation to COBOL. However, the concepts of structured design are useful for all high-level languages, including APL, RPGII, and RPGIII, as well as assemblers, macro assemblers, and machine language.

Others who may find these concepts helpful are supervisors, managers of programmers and analysts, and programmers who will be producing or maintaining programs that have been designed using structured design. Hobbyists and those with home computers, while not typically so concerned with reducing the cost and time of developing programs, may find the concepts of structured design useful for generating flexible and changeable programs as well as for taking advantage of reusable code.

Since this book is oriented primarily toward enhancing the ability to *use* structured design, tips, techniques, and examples for using structured design constitute its primary focus. The concepts of structured design necessary for its productive use in everyday work are included here. However, the rigor, preciseness, and depth that would be necessary to present the *theory* of structured design adequately have deliberately been avoided. In this way, those who wish to make use of structured design can do so without taking the time necessary to study the theory in its entirety. Readers interested in a complete description of the theory of structured design are referred to the book by Yourdon and Constantine in the bibliography.

2
Introduction to Structured Design

Structured design is a set of concepts, measurements, and guidelines whose purpose is to reduce the cost of developing and maintaining computer programs. The costs associated with people are a major part of the cost of developing and maintaining programs. These costs can be reduced by reducing the complexity people have to deal with. Structured design is a technique which reduces complexity. Another major advantage of structured design is that it facilitates making changes, both to fix an error and to implement a new requirement. Possibly the most important benefit of structured design, though, is that it greatly enhances the ability to *reuse* code.

Structured design is a technique for separating functions within a program into relatively independent modules. Why such a division produces benefits will be explained below. The technique of separating functions that together accomplish some larger objective is already in widespread use in other industries. The component parts of a car, an airplane, or a house and the interface between these functional components is so well defined that they can be (and typically are) designed, manufactured, and improved by different people or companies. Moreover, the component parts (or copies of them) are often used in other designs. These advantages are not currently enjoyed in the data process-

3

ing industry when programs are implemented as single monolithic pieces.

The technique of modularity is, in fact, not new to computer programming either. The technique has been used for a long time, although with different objectives and thus with different results. (Refer to "Coincidental Binding" in Chapter 5.)

Research Showed That It Worked

Structured design is based on empirical research done by Larry Constantine. This research was started in 1962, probably predating most, if not all, of the "Improved Programming Techniques." Constantine noticed that some programs were less costly to produce and maintain than others. He gathered data on many different programs in order to determine what characteristic seemed to be associated with those programs observed to be less costly to produce and maintain. He observed that programs that were the least costly to develop and maintain generally were implemented as modular structures. Moreover, certain kinds of modular structures reduced the cost more than others. Thus, the concept of structured design was developed.

Why It Works

In order to more fully understand the technique of structured design it is useful to examine why the use of modular structures tends to reduce the cost of developing and maintaining programs. Problem solving is harder when all aspects of a problem are considered simultaneously. It is easier if a way can be found to solve relatively independent pieces of the problem one by one.

In programming terms, it is generally true that doubling the size of a program more than doubles the time necessary to implement it. There is some indication that doubling the size of a program makes it four times as hard to implement (a relationship roughly like that shown in the chart in Figure 2.1). For our purposes here, it is sufficient if doubling the program size at least more than doubles the time necessary to implement it. For example, compare a one-page program to a two-page program. Both pages of the two-page program must be coded, already consuming twice the time of a single-page program. In the two-page program, however, some *extra* time is needed in order to make the two pages work correctly with each other.

If doubling the size of a program more than doubles the time

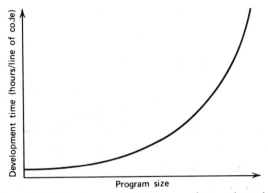

Figure 2.1 Development time grows faster than size.

necessary to implement it, then developing a program as two pices than than one reduces the total effort (if the pieces are relatively independent). Additional benefits can be achieved by dividing the resulting pieces. Benefits accrue until every piece contains only one function. Dividing single functions into pieces yeleds *dependent* pieces, which makes them harder, not easier, to work with. There is a correct number of modules that minimizes the complexity for any particular program (Figure 2.2)

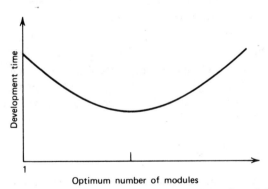

Figure 2.2 There is an optimum number of modules.

The Goal of Structured Design

The goal of structured design is to design programs as structures of independent, single-function modules. Independent, because this achieves the benefit of solving each part of the problem piece by piece. Single-function, because that is how the maximum benefit is achieved. The resulting program turns out to be easier to develop and maintain. Other characteristics are the following:

- The program is simpler: it can be understood, checked, programmed, debugged, fixed, and changed piece by piece.
- Modules can be programmed relatively independently.
- The program can be understood piece by piece.
- People are less likely to make errors, because less code has to be dealt with at a time.
- Testing is easier, because the program can be tested piece by piece.
- Less code has to be considered in order to implement changes.
- Side effects of changes are drastically reduced.
- Personnel changes are less critical, since the programmers are involved with smaller pieces of code at any one time.
- The division of code into one-page segments as required by structured programming is nearly complete.
- The functional decomposition which HIPO (Hierarchy plus Input Process Output) uses to document a program is complete.
- More accurate cost estimates are possible, because estimating is improved when estimates are made on many smaller pieces.
- Optimization efforts can be applied to critical areas. (This is dealt with in Chapter 11, "Structured Design and Performance.")
- Single-function modules are uniquely qualified to be used in future programs. This single advantage probably constitutes the most important reason for using structured design. It will be dealt with in the last two chapters of the book.

Where Structured Design Fits

Structured design is specifically a *program* design technique. It is a very advantageous step to go through after system design, that is, once the programs, their objectives, and the format of all input and output data have been decided. It is done prior to the detailed program design, where the decisions are made as to how to implement the requirements of the program in code.

Structured design is not a comprehensive system design technique, since it will not aid in file design, input and output layout, choice of access method, operating environment, hardware or software, and so forth. On the other hand, the concepts included in structured design can be very useful during system design. Structured design can definitely be used on programs specified to include multiple objectives. Structured design concepts do, however, indicate that the flexibility, usability, and changeability of *programs* is, as with modules, are enhanced when each program is designed to achieve a single specific objective. Thus, the concepts of structured design can be extremely useful in systems design for producing flexible, changeable systems by avoiding multiple, unrelated functions in a single program.

Many companies are organized so that design is often done by an analyst, and the results are passed over to the programming group for implementation. Since structured design is a technique that lies right between the functions of these two groups, the question of who should do it arises. The author's opinion is that it is much more beneficial to have the analyst do the structured design. The knowledge needed to do the best structured design is a good understanding of the user requirements, design alternatives, and likely changes that may impact the system. Typically, the analyst knows these better than the programmer.

Furthermore, the result of the structured design process is a much more concise and specific statement of the objectives of the program than the system design documentation is. Thus the structured design documentation constitutes a simple, flexible, understandable interface between the analyst and the programmers. Structure charts resulting from structured design depict more clearly what is otherwise often passed to programmers in the form of program narratives. Detailed module specifications, input and output definitions, and file designs also need to be part of the design documentation.

Its Relationship to Other Techniques

Since the advantages of structured design rely on modularity, it is compatible with structured programming, HIPO, and top-down development. Structured programming requires one-in/one-out single-page segments. Structured programming does not, however, include a technique for choosing segmentation. Structured design provides a reasoning behind, and a mechanism for, choosing the segmentation in such a way that the advantage from segmentation is maximized. Thus, while structured programming suggests writing programs in segments (regardless of how the program was designed, documented, or is to be implemented), structured design shows how to produce the most independent segments.

Similarly, HIPO suggests that programs be documented in functional pieces, whether or not the design, programming, and/or implementation is being done in pieces. Structured design is a way to design those functional pieces at a program level. Top-down development assumes modules exist when it suggests implementing modules from the top downwards in the structure.

Use of any of the above techniques separately will achieve some of the benefits of modularity. Together, they dovetail for a consistent approach that maximizes the benefits to be achieved from modularity. While structured design does, in some sense, enhance an environment that includes structured analysis, development support library, walkthroughs, and chief programmer teams, the term *compatibility* is probably not appropriate. Structured design certainly is not incompatible with these techniques. It is simply that the techniques referred to apply to different areas of the effort, which have little to do with modularity directly. While certain advantages can be discerned, such as the advantage in walkthroughs of being able to walk through smaller independent pieces, these are minor benefits compared to the major dovetailing of structured design with structured programming, HIPO, and top-down development.

Structured design needs program specifications as input. It can follow any technique that produces program specifications. In particular, structured analysis produces good input for structured design.

The output of structured design is a structure chart that should be augmented with module specifications. Thus, structured design can provide input to any technique for writing code, such as traditional coding, a program specification language, or pseudocode.

The use of code generation techniques that produce code based on the structure of the data is better done after structured design. Such approaches reduce the complexity of program development when related to traditional design and coding methods. However, the data structure analysis step, which these techniques require first, still gets exponentially more complex as the program gets bigger. As discussed above, structured design helps to flatten this exponential curve. Thus, as the program gets bigger it becomes more and more important to do structured design first. Also, specifications are not always complete and precise, they change as programs are being developed, and programs would still need to change even if they were error free. Structured design produces code in a way that allows code to be adapted to changes as they occur. Thus structured design is an important step to take for all programs.

Summary

Structured design reduces the cost of developing and maintaining programs by reducing the time and effort required. It does so by reducing complexity and by making it easier to implement changes—both to fix an error and to add a new requirement. Structured design is a technique for producing a result that is a combination of relatively independent, interrelated functional units. This technique is used in the development of products in virtually every other industry. The technique of modularity itself is not even new to programming. But previous objectives and, thus, the results have been very different from those achieved with structured design.

Structured design is based on empirical research, done by Larry Constantine, into what caused some programs to be less costly to produce and maintain than others. He found that those programs observed to be easier to develop and maintain typically were modular.

The reason structured design works is related to a characteristic of problem solving in general. Problem solving is harder when all aspects of the problem are considered simultaneously. It is easier if the problem can be solved piece by piece. This characteristic shows up in programming in that doubling the size of a program usually more than doubles the time necessary to implement it. Thus, designing the program as two pieces rather than one can reduce the total effort, if the pieces are relatively independent. Additional benefits are derived by dividing the resulting pieces again and again, until each piece contains only one function.

The goal, then, of structured design is to design a program as a structure of independent single-function modules. The resulting program turns out to be easier to develop and maintain. In addition, it has the following characteristics:

- The program is simpler.
- The program can be written, understood, tested, and changed piece by piece.
- People are less likely to make errors.
- Side effects of changes are drastically reduced.

- Personnel changes are less critical.
- More accurate cost estimates are possible.
- Optimization efforts can be applied to critical areas.
- Single-function modules are uniquely qualified to be used in future programs.

Structured design is a program design technique. It is a very valuable step that is done after system design and before the programming step. But structured design concepts can also be a useful technique during systems design for enhancing the flexibility, usability, and changeability of systems of programs. In an environment where analysts turn over their results to programmers, the analysts have the best information for doing structured design. Having the analysts do the structured design also results in a more concise description of the objectives when they are turned over to the programmers.

Because of the modularity of structured design, it is compatible with structured programming, HIPO, and top-down development. It can be used in conjunction with structured analysis, development support library, walk-throughs, inspections, and chief programer teams. Structured design can take program specifications from any source including structured analysis. The resulting structure chart, augmented with module specifications, is good input for traditional coding, a program specification language, or pseudocode. Techniques which produce code based on data structure should be done after structured design to get the benefit of the bigger reduction in complexity and the more changeable code produced by structured design.

3

Structured Design Concepts

The Definition of a Module

A module is a set of program statements that can be invoked by a name. The following are some examples:

- Separately compiled programs
- COBOL paragraphs or sections
- PL/1 procedures
- FORTRAN subroutines
- Assembler macros
- Structured Programming segments (achieved by any method)

The concepts of structured design can be applied to all of these (and other) environments. One objective of modularity, however, is to enable the pieces of the program to be dealt with relatively independently. Modules are more independent if each has its own distinct set of variable names. For most languages, this is achieved by separate compiles (note that internal procedures in PL/1 do not suffice, since they allow referencing the local variables of the enclosing procedure).

The mechanism used to invoke separately compiled programs in most languages is the CALL statement. The use of the CALL statement does not imply that the module *must* be fetched from an external storage medium into memory each time it is executed. While this type of dynamic loading may be a desirable option in some cases, it is not a necessary requirement in order to achieve the benefits of structured design. The result of the CALL statement is equivalent to the COBOL PERFORM statement, with the exception that parameters are passed. The performance difference between this type of static CALL and a PERFORM statement is negligible (despite the general impression that a CALL statement adds a lot of overhead). A complete discussion of the subject, including the results of performance measurements, is given in Chapter 11, "Structured Design and Performance."

Coupling and Binding

Two measurements are of interest relative to achieving independence between modules. The primary measure is coupling. Coupling measures the strength of relationships between modules (Figure 3.1). The objective is to maximize independence by minimizing coupling. The second and complementary measure is binding (Figure 3.2). Binding measures the strength of relationship between elements of code within a module.

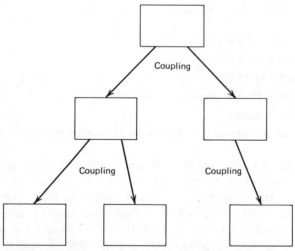

Figure 3.1 Coupling measures the strength of relationships between modules.

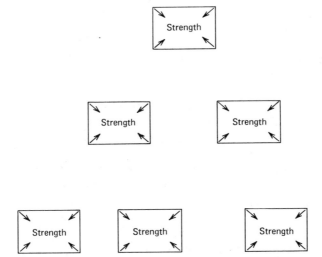

Figure 3.2 Binding measures the strength of relationships within a module.

Actually, coupling and binding measure opposite aspects of the same thing. All programs have elements of code that are highly related. If these are placed into separate modules, the modules will be highly coupled. The objective is to place highly related elements of code in the same module so that there is low coupling between modules.

Usually, binding is considered first in order to create an initial modular structure such that highly related elements are in the same module. Next, the resulting coupling is minimized by looking for alternatives that will reduce the coupling between the modules even further. While the order is basically to maximize the binding first and then minimize the module coupling, the binding and coupling concepts can be used throughout the process. However, the primary measure and intent is to reduce the module coupling, since this is the direct measure of how independent the modules are.

Summary

The benefits of structured design result from the independence of the modules. Modules are more independent if they have the ability to define local variables that are not available to any other parts of the program. Thus, for programming in assembler or higher-level languages, the most independent modules are separately compiled. Separately compiled modules are usually invoked by a CALL statement, (which does not require dynamic loading.)Calls are resolved by the linkage editor. At execution time the result is equivalent to a PER-FORM statement, with the exception that parameters are passed. (The difference in execution time of the resulting program is difficult even to detect.)

Two major measurements are of interest in order to evaluate alternatives for modular structures. The primary one is coupling, which is the measure of relationships between modules. The objective is to achieve the maximum independence, in other words, the lowest coupling. The second and complementary measure is binding, which measures the dependence between elements of code. Since all programs have elements of code that are highly related, it is helpful to identify these and to group them into the same module. If dependent elements of code are in different modules, the *modules* will be highly related. The concepts of binding and coupling actually measure the same thing from two different points of view.

The technique suggested in this book for doing structured design is to build an initial structure based primarily on binding. Then look for ways to improve the structure, typically through reducing the resulting coupling.

4

Structure Charts

The Symbols

To facilitate the structured design process, a structure chart is drawn to display the binding and coupling characteristics of the modules. A structure chart uses familiar flowcharting symbols in a slightly new way. The familiar rectangle represents a module. The name of the module is shown starting in the upper lefthand corner of the rectangle. The name is the simple phrase (or acronym for it) that describes the function of the module. An arrow from module A to module B, as in Figure 4.1, indicates that module A contains one or more CALLs to module B. The term CALL used here refers to any mechanism used to invoke a module. In the case of separately compiled modules, it usually is the CALL statement itself. In the case of paragraphs, it may be a PERFORM statement. In the case of assembler macros, APL, and FORTRAN subroutine subfunctions, it can be simply the inclusion of the module's name in an expression.

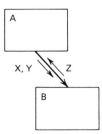

Figure 4.1 Module A calls module B.

The arrow indicating the CALL is always annotated with the parameters that are passed. These annotations also indicate the direction in which data is passed. In Figure 4.1, X and Y contain data that A passes to B. Z contains data B passes back to A. If a parameter is used to pass data to B that B updates and returns, then that parameter is shown in both sets. This is true even though that parameter will appear only once within the CALL statement. While it is somewhat more readable to have the parameters going to B on the left of the CALL arrow and the parameters returning from B on the right, room on the chart does not always permit it, nor is it really necessary. Parameters may appear on either side of the call arrow, or both may appear on the same side, since the direction of data being passed is indicated by the direction of the annotation arrow.

The parameter names shown on the chart are those used within the module containing the CALL statement (module A). While clarity and understanding are typically improved by using the same name for the same parameter among all modules, there are many situations where different names enhance clarity and understanding, as in Figure 4.2. (The example of the module ADD is not intended to be an example of a good module, but rather to illustrate the point of clarity of parameter names). The reason the caller's names for the parameters are used is that the caller's names will be at least as clear as, and often clearer than, the called program's names for them. (In Figure 4.2, the parameter names inside ADD are probably at best something obscure like X, Y, and SUM). For final documentation, a form as in the structure chart shown in Figure 4.3 can be used. Each unique interface is numbered. The parameters are then shown in a table somewhere on the same page or on an attached page. The table indicates which parameters are used as input parameters to the called module and which ones are output

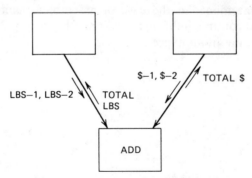

Figure 4.2 Parameter names are those used by the caller.

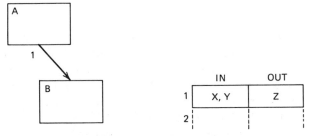

Figure 4.3 Module A calls module B.

from the called module to the caller. Parameters updated by the called module and returned appear in both columns. While this form is useful for final documentation, it should never be used while designing a structure chart. Putting the parameters in a table separates the parameters from the connection that they document. This physically separates highly related things which makes the design process more difficult.

The addition of some procedural annotations turns out to be extremely useful and informative. In Figure 4.4, module A conditionally calls module B. Module A also calls either C, D, or neither. In Figure 4.5, module A repetitively calls modules B and C. Also, the "1" indicates that module A calls module D only once. The "1" does not indicate one call to D each time A is executed; that is what an arrow depicts.

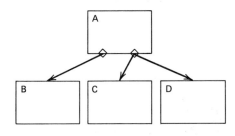

Figure 4.4 Conditional calls.

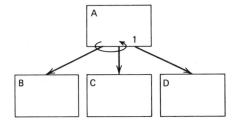

Figure 4.5 Iterative and once-only calls.

These conditional and looping annotations are optional. Also, they cannot always be entirely rigorous. This is because the procedural aspects may differ, depending on the data received by A. For example, end-of-file conditions or error processing may change the normal procedural aspects. The most useful way to use the procedural annotations is to indicate the *normally* expected procedure of A, in the absence of either end-of-file (EOF) or error conditions.

Thus, although the presence of procedural annotations indicates the presence of said function, their absence does not guarantee the absence of such conditions or loops.

Double bars down the side of the rectangle indicate a predefined module, as in Figure 4.6. This is a module that has already been written and debugged and whose object and source modules are available in a module library.

The arrow in Figure 4.7 denotes a connection from *inside* A to *inside* B. This occurs when module A contains a reference to a location defined within B. (See "Types of Connections" in Chapter 6 for an example.) The arrow points toward the item being referenced. Data or control may pass either way.

Figure 4.6   A predefined module.

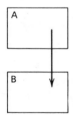

Figure 4.7   A reference from within A to within B.

Parallel activation (e.g., ATTACH) of B by A is indicated by a dotted arrow, as in Figure 4.8. Control may or may not return to the next sequential instruction in A. A macro is indicated by a dotted rectangle, as in Figure 4.9. The symbol in Figure 4.10 represents the operating system. It can be used to show that the operating system calls the top module in a structure or that modules within the structure call the operating system to perform certain services, such as I/O.

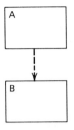

Figure 4.8 Parallel activation.

Figure 4.9 A macro.

Figure 4.10 The operating system.

Comments can be added by using the symbol shown in Figure 4.11. Use it sparingly, though, to avoid overcomplicating the structure chart. Avoid using it to add "how-to" comments to the chart; put these in the module descriptions.

Additional symbols are defined for the complete charting technique (Yourdon and Constantine, 1979). The ones included here are those needed for doing structured design in today's typical application development environment.

Charting Techniques

It is useful to place modules on a chart in such a way as to minimize the crossing of lines. Once this is accomplished, it is useful if modules are placed in the most likely order of execution: from left to right. It is not, however, incorrect to place them in other orders.

It is important that a given module never appear more than once on a chart. This is because as improvements are made to a structure,

Figure 4.11 Comments.

parameters and functions may change. If there are multiple copies of a given module on the chart, it is possible to change the parameters or function of one copy of the module and not another. Thus, a change may be made that is not justified. The error is not discovered, the programmer implementing the module will have a rather difficult time implementing it!

If a module is used from many locations, use a small circular connector, as in Figure 4.12, showing the called module once within the structure, or alternately at the edge of the page or on an attached page. This can be especially useful for utility modules. If the parameters are always the same, they can be shown with the utility module, as in Figure 4.12. Otherwise, show them with each call.

When drawing structure charts, try to show as much of the chart as possible on the same piece of paper. Always show at least three levels together. Spreading a structure chart across many pieces of paper adds unnecessary complexity. This is because people have to concentrate on putting the struture chart together mentally in order to work with it.

There are several ways to get more of the structure chart on each piece of paper. Use a template with a smaller rectangle than the standard flowcharting template. Use large paper, such as computer printer paper. This chart can then be copied on a reducing copier. Use two or even four sheets, if necessary. Using two sheets sideways and end

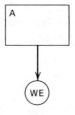

Figure 4.12 A connector.

to end can often allow another level, since it is usually the width rather than the height which limits the number of levels. A multiple-sheet chart can be copied by copying each sheet and taping the copies together. This is easier than trying to put the chart together mentally all the time. The use of connectors (see Figure 4.12) for utility modules also reduces the number of rectangles needing to fit side by side on any level of the structure chart.

Doing the design on a large blackboard makes it easy to make changes. If this is done, it may be useful to take a picture of it every day with an instant camera.

Figure 4.13 shows an example of a complete structure chart. Each rectangle indicates a separately compiled module. The chart shows calls from module to module, parameters, the direction the data is passed, as well as procedural annotations of conditional and looping calls.

Structure Charts Relative to Other Charts

Structure charts are intended to be developed *prior* to producing code. However, you can understand what a structure chart is by considering a case in which the code for all the modules is already written. You could

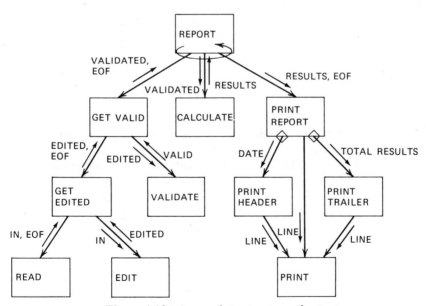

Figure 4.13 A complete structure chart.

then draw a structure chart by taking any module, drawing a box for it, and putting its name in the box. You would then inspect the code of the module to detect any modules which it calls and draw rectangles for those modules and arrows from the original module to each of the called modules indicating the parameters beside the arrow. Next, inspect the called modules for further called modules, repeating the procedure above. Continue until all modules have been inspected and the chart shows all calls. The result is a structure chart.

A structure chart is similar to, and can replace, a HIPO hierarchy chart (to the extent that the latter documents code), except that the HIPO hierarchy chart does not document the interface parameters. Also, which (of many) functional breakdowns the HIPO chart shows is arbitrary.

A structure chart is *not* a flowchart. A flowchart shows the procedural aspects of a program. It indicates which part executes first, next, and so on. The structure chart is, instead, a "responsibility" chart. It is much more like an organization chart for a company. An organization chart shows who reports to whom, rather than who comes to work first in the morning. While, admittedly, the top module in a structure chart does in fact get control first, structure charts typically pass control almost immediately through the structure to a module at the bottom. Then, each module completes its function on the return route up through the structure. In these cases, the completion of the execution of each function is in exactly the opposite order as would be implied if the structure chart were considered to be a flowchart. Also, notice that the arrow denoting the CALL implies automatic return to the next sequential instruction when the called module exits. In contrast, the arrows in a flowchart imply no such return.

A structure chart is, in fact, somewhat like a sideways view of a flowchart. The modules contain sections of logic that are segmented out of what might otherwise be a complete flowchart for the entire program. This process is a familiar one to those who have done segmentation for Structured Programming. In that process, however, the segments typically are pictured as being brought out to the right. Once such a structure is turned 90 degrees clockwise and parameters are added to the connections, it is, in fact, a structure chart (Figure 4.14).

Summary

A structure chart is drawn to display the binding and coupling in a structure of modules. The familiar flowcharting rectangle is used to

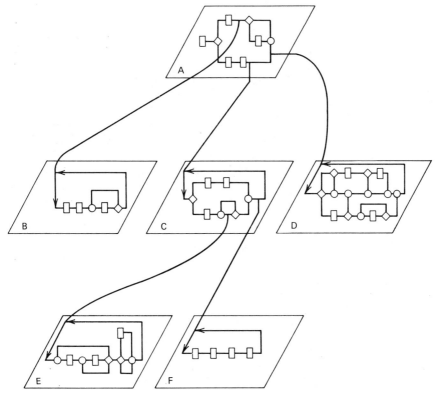

Figure 4.14   Structure charts versus flowcharts.

indicate a module. The module name—the function of a module—is put within the rectangle and can be used to identify the binding. An arrow from one module to another indicates that the first module contains one or more CALLs to the second. The arrow is annotated with the parameters that are passed. These annotations show for each parameter which way the designer intends to have the data flow.

Procedural annotations are added to indicate conditional calls, loops around calls, and modules that are called only once. Other symbols indicate modules that are available in the module library, parallel activation (e.g., ATTACH), and macros.

Charting techniques include avoiding crossing of lines and, where possible, placing modules in likely order of execution from left to right. Further, it is important that a given module never appear more than once on a chart. Circular connectors can be used for modules called from many places.

Show at least three levels of a structure chart together. Use a smaller template for the rectangles, larger paper, and two or four pages taped together. It is easier for others to tape pages together than constantly to have to put the structure together mentally.

A structure chart depicts the calling structure of the modules. It is not a flowchart. Instead, it is much more like an organization chart, which shows the relationships of organizational responsibilities. In fact, organizational responsibilities are typically very functional and independent, with the units combining to accomplish the overall goal or goals of the organization. These are also characteristics of good structure charts.

5

Binding

Binding measures the strength of relationships between elements of code within a module (Figure 5.1). The scale of binding is shown in Figure 5.2. Types of binding have been identified along what is actually a continuous scale. The points selected are not critical. The value of examining different points along the scale is to identify characteristics

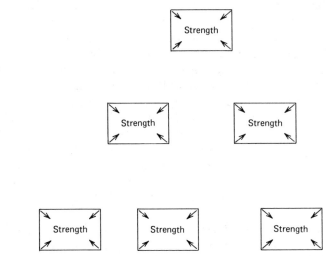

Figure 5.1   Binding measures the strength of relationships within a module.

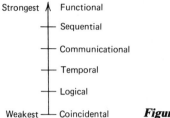

Figure 5.2 Binding.

of types of binding that are other than functional. The objective is to always have functional binding. Often a module's binding is made functional with a single change rather than through successive incremental improvements to the binding.

The scale of binding was derived by classifying responses received when programmers were asked, "Why were these elements of code put together?" One resulting characteristic of the scale is that the reasons for relationships at any level can also include reasons from levels below it. That is, the binding between elements of code is determined from the *strongest* relationship that applies, even if characteristics of weaker relationships are also exhibited.

Coincidental Binding

The anchor point on the scale is coincidental binding. Sometimes the answer to the question, why were the elements of code put together is "Well, they had to go some place." This is one way to view coincidental binding. In other words, there is no meaningful relationship between the programming elements; they just (coincidentally) happened to be together. Although these kinds of modules are probably seldom designed anymore, they used to result from tricks used to save memory. On the 1401, for example, memory was often so constrained that anything which saved memory allowed more function to be included. One trick was to look for repeated sequences of instructions. If the instructions were longer than the linkage necessary to branch to them and back, memory could be saved each time they were reused.

Figure 5.3 shows an example of coincidental binding. The three instructions MOVE A TO B, READ CARD FILE, and MOVE C TO D have nothing to do with one another. A, B, C, and D are not on the card file, nor are A and B related to C or D. They are just three instructions that appeared more than once in a program. In fact, by getting really tricky, additional savings could be generated by noting

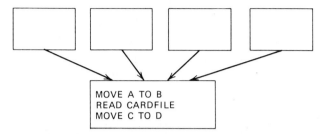

Figure 5.3 Coincidental binding.

that there were times when the code moved A to B and C to D, but did not read from the card file. Reading from the card file would, however, cause no problems at that point. So by inserting READ CARD FILE, some additional memory savings could be achieved. At another location there might be no need to move C to D, but again, doing so would not cause any problem.

The difficulties start when it turns out that one location does not need to move A to B, but needs to move A to E. An easy way to fix that is to set a switch. "If switch-1 is ON, move A to E; otherwise, move A to B." In order to avoid using a great deal of additional memory, the switch can be initialized to OFF at the beginning of the program. Then the switch is set to ON from that particular location before calling the module, and to OFF again after returning. Note the characteristic that if the location that generated the need for the switch makes a mistake, such as leaving the switch on, it will cause some *other* location to encounter an error. This is the antithesis of a major objective of structured design, which is to minimize the chance that errors in one module will cause a different module to fail.

After a number of similar changes, the program is finally debugged and put into production. Sometime later, a tape drive is added to the system. Now, certain locations that read from the card file need to read from the tape drive. The situation is handled as before: switch-26 says: "If ON, read from the tape drive; otherwise, read from the card file, but if switches 17 and 13 are ON, read from the card file anyway. And then move from C to D, unless switches 6, 8, and 14 are ON, in which case move from C to K, unless switch 2 is OFF, in which case move from C to J." It is no wonder that the maintenance programmer is reluctant to change the code at this point. It takes several weeks to get the program working again when any change is made. The maintenance programmer may also be convinced that at least five switches are no longer being used but would not dare eliminate them, just in case.

The problem with coincidental binding is that changes needed by one caller are often not needed by all callers. Contrast this to a functional module such as SQUARE ROOT. It is reasonable to assume that if one caller needs a change to SQUARE ROOT (because it was not operating properly), all callers will want the same change.

The objectives for modularity used by structured design result in modules that are functional. Their binding is at the exact opposite end of the scale from the coincidental modules that result from the objective of saving memory. In fact, the complexity which resulted from the latter kind of module was so great that this kind of modularity was usually avoided anyway as soon as there was sufficient memory, and justifiably so. But with the advent of mini and micro computers there are now new temptations to save memory with these coincidental modules again.

Logical Binding

The next type of binding is logical binding. Here, the elements perform a class of functions, typically using the same verb. Figure 5.4 shows a module with logical binding, which will edit all data. It edits master records, deletions, updates, or additions. The relationship between any element of code in one of these updates to any element of code in another is classified as a "logical" relationship, in other words, both elements perform the same type of function, but on different data. A typical characteristic of modules such as the one in Figure 5.4 is that code is shared between functions. In fact, this is often the reason given for these modules' creation. This presumed advantage will be examined below. Another characteristic of logical binding is that often the module starts with a multiway switch that branches to the portion of code to be executed. This is because the relationships between elements of code within the module are so weak that major portions of code are not even applicable each time the module is entered.

To see the problem with this kind of binding, take even the best case:

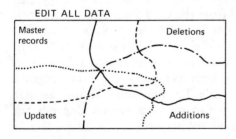

Figure 5.4 Logical binding.

everything works correctly. Suppose a change is to be made in how additions are edited. If the change is made in a portion of code overlapped between edit additions and edit updates, an error will be introduced, since there was no change specified for editing updates. In order to fix edit updates, a further change is required. If this change is made in code overlapped between edit updates and edit master records, an additional error is introduced. Fixing edit master records may change edit deletions. Fixing edit deletions may even introduce an error back into edit additions again, and so on. Although this particular chain of events is the worst case, when there are large amounts of code overlapped, there is a high probability that changes can cause new errors. This is especially true because it is usually difficult to identify which code is overlapped and what functions share the code.

Overlapping code does not save development or coding time, even though overlapping is often done on the assumption that it will save time. It always takes *extra* time. For example, in order to overlap code in the module in Figure 5.4 one must first decide how to edit additions, how to edit updates, and so on. It then takes *extra* time to determine what portions of the code can be overlapped. Time spent actually *writing* the overlapped code twice can be eliminated by using a copier. The time spent *deciding* how to write the overlapped code can also be eliminated through the use of a copier. Common functions, such as EDIT NAME FIELD, can be written as separate modules anyway and called from EDIT UPDATE and EDIT ADDITIONS. The only portions of overlapped code that remain are portions that just happen (coincidentally) to be the same today but may need to be different tomorrow. Overlapping the code will make it more difficult to change one function without changing the other. Thus, the technique of overlapping code is only a memory-saving technique which takes *extra* time to write and is *harder* to change. This is one of many cases where the programmer can actually spend *more* time writing code that is *harder* to maintain!

Temporal Binding

The next level on the scale of binding, although still very weak, is temporal binding—time-related. Here the strongest relationship between elements of code is that they are all executed at the same time. Examples are modules that get all the program's data now, do clean-up, housekeeping, termination, or initialization. A module that edits all fields in a record is temporally bound rather than only logically bound because the elements all execute at the same time—since all the data is available at the same time.

Temporal binding is slightly higher on the scale than logical binding because all the elements in a temporally bound module can potentially execute every time the module is invoked. It is also somewhat simpler than logical binding because it does not need a multiway switch. A module such as an initialization module can have temporal binding with a logical relationship between the elements of code; in this case, the elements have the same verb *and* all execute at the same time. This is a stronger binding than temporal binding where the elements are not logically related. The purpose here, however, is not to classify all types of modules, but rather to note the characteristics of modules that are not functionally bound in order to identify modules which can be improved.

Communicational Binding

The next types of binding are considerably stronger than previous ones. These are the first types of binding where elements of code reference the same data. The two ways this can happen are called communicational binding and sequential binding. Making the distinction between these types of binding is less important than being able to determine the presence of either one.

The weaker of the two is communicational binding. Here, the elements only reference the same input and/or output data, as in Figure 5.5. Elements that produce multiple reports from the same stream of data are communicationally bound. So are elements that both print and store an input data item. Also, elements that update and delete a given

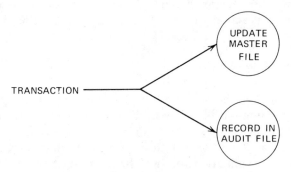

Figure 5.5 Communicational binding.

record in a file are communicationally bound to each other. Communicational binding is a slightly weaker relationship than sequential binding, because the elements of code typically can execute in either order.

Sequential Binding

Sequential Binding is when the output data from one element is the input for the next, as in Figure 5.6. This relationship is slightly stronger than communicational binding because one element depends on the previous for the data. Examples are elements that get and edit some data; elements that create and store a record in a file; and elements which accumulate results and print them. Modularizing a flowchart usually produces sequentially bound modules.

Functional Binding

Functional binding is at the top of the scale. It is probably easier to understand than it is to define. One definition is "elements combined to accomplish a single specific task. A functionally bound module is one that contains all the elements, and only those elements, necessary to accomplish a single specific task. While this may define functional binding, it raises the question of what a single specific objective is. The following examples of functionally bound modules may help to illustrate the concept:

- SQUARE ROOT
- GET DATE
- PROCESS HOURLY PAYROLL
- CALCULATE DEDUCTIONS
- CALCULATE SOCIAL SECURITY
- PRINT CHECK

Figure 5.6 Sequential binding.

Note that although some of these modules are probably bottom level, others are higher in the structure. Functionality is a concept that can be applied at all levels within the structure. For example, PROCESS HOURLY PAYROLL calls a number of modules, including CALCU-LATE DEDUCTIONS, which itself calls CALCULATE SOCIAL SECURITY.

A Mechanical Example

The concept of functional binding can be further illustrated by means of a mechanical example of an engine, as depicted in Figure 5.7. (The charting technique used is a hierarchical one, since it shows a relation-ship among parts rather than a CALL from one part to another.) The engine of a car consists of many parts, among them a water pump, carburetor, and fuel pump. The carburetor consists of many parts. Among them a valve, an automatic choke, and an accelerator pump. Each block on the chart has a single function. The engine's function is to provide power for the car. The function of the water pump is to pump water. The carburetor's function is to mix fuel and air. The fuel pump's function is to pump fuel. The automatic choke's function is to adjust the fuel/air mixture based on the temperature of the engine.

   One characteristic of a functional unit is that it can easily be replaced by any other element that will serve the same purpose. For

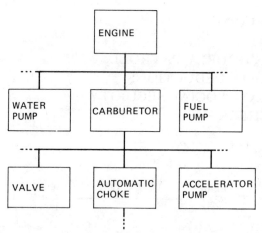

Figure 5.7   A mechanical example of functional binding.

example, the engine can be replaced by any other engine that will also provide power to the car, such as a turbine engine or an electric engine. Similarily, a carburetor can be replaced by any other mechanism that properly mixes fuel and air. The automatic choke is already a replacement for the old hand chokes.

Another characteristic of functional pieces is that there are simple connections between them and their surroundings. For example, the carburetor needs to input only fuel, air, and the temperature of the car, and passes the fuel and air mixture out. The water pump needs water in, water out, and a power source.

Consider the divisions of the engine that are not functional, for example, one half of a carburetor. There is no way to describe adequately the *one* thing that half of a carburetor does. It does not do any *one* thing. In fact, it cannot do anything unless matched with its exact other half. The other half of any other carburetor will not suffice. The linkage between the two halves of a carburetor is highly complex and very dependent upon the particular carburetor.

It *is* true that if parts are eliminated from half of a carburetor, the eventual result can be an automatic choke, which is functional. But there is no way to describe the function of half of a carburetor in such a way as to include a description of what all the parts are doing, without describing multiple things.

On the other hand, if the breakdown is such that one result is a carburetor–water pump combination, again there is no single way to describe what the unit does. It both pumps water and mixes fuel and air. Any attempt to describe the complete function will inevitably include an AND, a comma, or some other mechanism for including two ideas in a sentence. If more parts are added, the eventual result is an engine, which is functional. But these two pieces alone are not functional.

Note that although functionality can guide the decomposition at all levels within the structure, it does not dictate when to stop the decomposition process. It is true that functional modules can generally be decomposed into further subfunctions. How and when the decomposition process should be stopped is discussed in Chapter 7.

Identifying Functional Binding

One good way to determine if modules are functionally bound (i.e., contain only a single function) is to write a phrase fully describing what the module does. Analysis of the phrase can indicate whether or not the module is functionally bound. The module is not functionally bound if, in order to describe adequately what the module does, you need one of the following:

- *A compound sentence* such as EDIT CUSTOMER NAME AND ADDRESS.

- *More than one phrase* EDIT CUSTOMER NAME, ADDRESS (eliminates the AND but not the problem).

- *More than one verb* such as GET AND EDIT THE MASTER RECORD.

- *Words relating to time* such as INITIALIZATION or TERMI-NATION.

- *Words such as "housekeeping" or "clean-up"* These imply temporal binding.

- *A predicate that is not a single specific object* such as in EDIT ALL DATA. The lack of a single specific object usually indicates logical binding.

- *A non-specific verb* such as handle usually implies multiple functions.

A functionally bound module can always be described in a sentence with multiple phrases; such as, *input a number, take the square root of it, and return the result.* The key is the *necessity* of using techniques like those in the list above in order to describe nonfunctional modules completely.

The description of a module's function should include everything that occurs between the point when the module is called and the point when it returns to its caller. This is in contrast to describing the function of the code *within* the module. For example, Figure 5.8 depicts a module which, when passed a command, will have it processed. From the caller's point of view, it is irrelevant whether PROCESS COM-

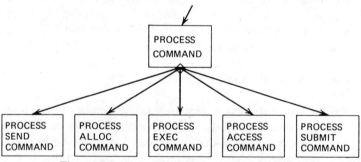

Figure 5.8 Accomplishment versus contents.

MAND is a single module or a structure—the function is the same. The reason for calling the module is to get a command processed. The description of the function *within* PROCESS COMMAND might be "DECIDE THE TYPE OF COMMAND AND PASS IT ALONG TO THE APPROPRIATE MODULE." However, this is a much less useful description of a module than is the name PROCESS COMMAND. The latter describes much more accurately the function desired by a caller that has a command to be processed.

The concept of functional binding is dependent on the data to be processed. Take, for example, a module EDIT CUSTOMER NAME AND ADDRESS. In a company where name and address are treated, edited, kept, and handled as two separate items, a module that edited the name and address would not be functionally bound. It would typically include either two segments of code (one to edit each item), overlapped code (where the editing happened to be similar today but could change tomorrow), or combinations of both overlapped and unique code. On the other hand, in a company that uses name and address simply to create mailing labels, name and address may be one single entry. Typically, there will also be a single name for it, such as "label data." In such a company, name and address would be expected to have a single editing requirement that would change consistently for both. In fact, there may not even be a clear distinction between where name stops and the address begins. For example, name may be one line and address four lines. The preceding example illustrates why testing for functionality by writing a description for the module is probably more useful than any definition of functionality could be (since it is unlikely that a definition could distinguish the difference indicated above).

Names for Modules

The preceeding section describes how to test for functionality by inspecting a phrase that describes what the module does, from its caller's point of view. This phrase makes a clear, descriptive, and useful name for the module. If this phrase is longer than that allowed for module names, an abbreviation or acronym can be used, in which case it is helpful if the complete phrase is included at the beginning of the prologue. An alphabetic name that describes the module's function makes it easier to understand and remember what each module does. This can help substantially to make the program easier to understand, check, debug, and change.

It is unfortunate to lose these advantages through the use of naming conventions that require numeric names for modules or that use valuable character positions in the name for much more mundane purposes (such as identifying the project which created the module). The purported reason for numeric names is to reduce the chance of synonyms. In order to eliminate synonyms, however, one must carefully keep track of all names used previously. But such a mechanism is also sufficient to eliminate synonyms in alphabetic names! In fact, letters increase the number of variations allowed in each character position, and thus *decrease* the mathematical chance of synonyms. Keeping modules in project libraries rather than in a common library can also reduce the chance of synonyms. The library index can still reference all available modules and point to the project library they are in. Even if one is compelled as a last resort to use numeric names for *some* functions, those functions are no more complex to use and understand than if *all* names were required to be numeric.

Module Binding

A module is functionally bound only if all possible pairs of elements within it exhibit a functional relationship. The binding is lowered by every pair of elements that does not exhibit functional binding. In order to identify nonfunctional modules and to indicate what is necessary to improve the binding, classify a module's binding as that of the lowest binding found within it. This simple classification scheme can not distinguish among all of the theoretically possible combinations of binding. But it is sufficient for the structured design process, with the following proviso. The binding of a module is improved when any nonfunctionally bound element(s) are removed, whether or not the module's binding changes on the basis of this simple classification scheme.

In practice, nonfunctional modules typically will have only two or three subfunctions within them. Any pair of elements from different subfunctions will exhibit other than functional binding. See Figure 5.9.

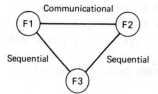

Figure 5.9 Nonfunctional subfunctions.

Eliminating any of the subfunctions improves the binding of the module. For example, eliminating subfunction F3 from the module in Figure 5.9 still leaves the module classified as communicationally bound. Its binding is improved, however, because some elements that were not functionally bound to others within the module have been removed. The module becomes functional after any two of the three subfunctions have been eliminated. Elimination of each of the subfunctions is an improvement independent of the order in which those changes are made.

Summary

Binding measures the strength of relationships between elements of code. It is a continuous relational scale. The objective is to have strong binding between all pairs of elements in each module. Identifying the types of binding along the scale allows evaluation of alternatives and helps identify characteristics of nonfunctionally bound modules. Nonfunctional modules can usually be made functional in a single step.

The weakest relationship is coincidental binding, which is when the elements "just happen to be together." Coincidentally bound modules used to result quite often from a memory-saving technique. Memory was saved by branching to a single copy of any sequence of code observed to occur more than once. Typically, however, changes wanted for one occurrence were not wanted by other occurrences. The result became more and more complex as switches were added to modify the execution for the callers' continually diverging requirements.

Logical binding is when elements perform a class of functions, typically using the same verb. An example is an EDIT RECORD module that will edit master records, deletions, updates, or additions. Typically, code is shared among the functions that edit each kind of record. Unfortunately, the shared code is often considered an *advantage*. The problem is that changes intended for only one of the functions may be made in an area of code that is shared with one of the other functions. In fact, since the boundaries of the shared areas are usually not clearly delineated, it can be difficult to avoid introducing unintentional errors into other functions. Changes intended to fix these errors can produce yet new errors, and so on. The irony is that it takes the programmer longer to decide how to overlap code between functions successfully than it does to simply duplicate or CALL portions of code needed more than once. This is one of a number of cases where a programmer spends *extra* time to produce code that is *harder* to maintain.

Temporal binding is when the strongest relationship between pairs of elements is that they execute at the same time. Temporal binding is a slightly stronger relationship than logical binding because the elements can all execute each time the module is called, whereas with logical binding, typically only one group of elements will execute at a time. Examples of temporal binding are modules that get all the program's data, do clean-up, housekeeping, termination, or initialization.

Communicational binding is when pairs of elements share the same input and/or output data, such as when they produce multiple reports from the same file. It is considerably stronger than previous types of binding, because for the first time the elements deal with the same data. The relationship is still somewhat weak, though, because the order in which they execute does not even matter.

Sequential binding is when output data from one element is input for the next, for example elements that accumulate results and print them. This relationship is slightly stronger than communicational binding because each element depends on the previous one for data and the order of execution is no longer optional.

Functional binding is when elements are combined to accomplish a single specific task. A functionally bound module contains all of the elements necessary to accomplish a single specific task. Examples of functional modules are SQUARE ROOT, GET DATE, PRINT CHECK, CALCULATE SOCIAL SECURITY, CALCULATE DEDUCTIONS, and PROCESS HOURLY PAYROLL. The engine of a car illustrates the concept of functional binding. An engine consists of many parts. Each part is functional and its function can be described by a simple phrase. The engine provides power for the car, the carburetor mixes fuel and air, and the automatic choke adjusts the fuel/air mixture on the basis of the engine temperature. Functional pieces typically have well-defined, simple interfaces to the rest of the structure. For example, the carburetor needs to input only fuel, air, and the temperature of the car and outputs only the fuel and air mixture. As a result of these simple interfaces, functional pieces can be designed and implemented separately and then connected to the rest of the structure. They can also be used again in future assemblies.

Nonfunctional divisions, such as a half a carburetor, are highly connected to the parts of the structure—specifically, the other half of the carburetor. No other half of any other carburetor will work. The two halves should never be considered, designed, or changed independent of one another. Conversely, larger combinations, such as a carburetor–water pump combination, are not functional because they do not do one thing. While the basic problem lies in not gaining the benefit of implementing each of the functions separately, more often, in addition, combining functions results in the compromise of one function for the benefit of the other. The functions may also be designed in an interrelated way, making it more difficult to modify one function without affecting the other.

To determine if modules are functionally bound, write a phrase fully describing what the module does. Functionally bound modules can be described by a simple phrase with a single verb and a single object. AND's, commas, compound sentences, multiple phrases, multiple verbs, multiple objects, and words such as INITIALIZATION, TERMINATION, HOUSEKEEPING, CLEAN-UP, ACCOMPLISH, and HANDLE indicate that more than one thing is being done. The phrase to be tested is the one that describes what the module is responsible for—all that happens between when the module is called and when it returns to its caller (from its caller's point of view)—as opposed to a description of what the code *inside* the module does.

This phrase which describes the module's function, or a shortened acronym for it, makes an excellent name for the module. Good module names reduce the necessity of having to divert attention from code that calls a module to temporarily looking at the called module to identify what it does. This greatly enhances the ability to deal with modules independently. The common practice of using numeric names for modules is unfortunate. Using numeric names is supposedly justified on the basis of avoiding synonyms. But alphabetic names have *less* chance of duplication than do numeric ones! In fact, the check for potential duplication of an alphabetic name may uncover an existing module that already does the desired function.

When the module contains all the elements, and only those elements, necessary to accomplish a single specific task, it is functional. The binding of a module is lowered by every possible pairing of elements that does not exhibit functional binding. The binding of a module is classified as that of the lowest binding between any two elements found within it. This identifies modules that are not functionally bound until all nonfunctional elements have been removed.

6

Coupling

Coupling measures the strength of relationships between modules (see Figure 6.1). The objective of structured design is to minimize the coupling between modules, so that they will be as independent as possible. The lower the coupling, the less likely that other modules will

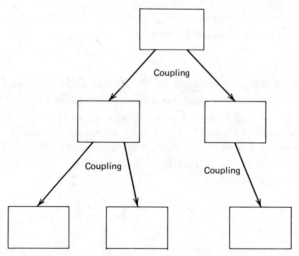

Figure 6.1   Coupling measures the strength of relationships between modules.

have to be considered in order to understand, fix, or change a given module.

Connections

Coupling primarily results from connections. A connection exists when an element of code references a location in memory defined elsewhere. In more general terms, a connection exists when two elements of code reference the same location in memory, usually to share a data item.

Figure 6.2 shows some structured COBOL code. Line 6 is connected to line 4 because both reference the location TRANS-RECORD. The connection is two-way; that is, line 6 is connected to line 4 by TRANS-

```
VALIDATE—TRANSACTION.
        MOVE 'YES' TO VALID—TRANS—FLAG.
        IF STOCK—NUMBER OF TRANS—RECORD IS NOT NUMERIC
            OR DATE—LIMIT OF TRANS—RECORD IS NOT NUMERIC
        THEN
            MOVE CORRESPONDING TRANS—RECORD TO MESSAGE—RECORD
            MOVE NOT—NUMERIC—MSG TO MESSAGE—FIELD
            MOVE MESSAGE—RECORD TO OUTPUT—LINE
            PERFORM LINE—OUT
            MOVE 'NO' TO VALID—TRANS—FLAG
        ELSE
            IF DATE—LIMIT OF TRANS—RECORD IS LESS THAN '70001'
            THEN
                MOVE CORRESPONDING TRANS—RECORD TO MESSAGE—RECORD
                MOVE DATE—LIMIT—MSG TO MESSAGE—FIELD
                MOVE MESSAGE—RECORD TO OUTPUT—LINE
                PERFORM LINE—OUT
                MOVE 'NO' TO VALID—TRANS—FLAG.
```

Figure 6.2   COBOL code.

RECORD and line 4 is connected to line 6 by TRANS-RECORD. Also, both line 4 and line 6 are connected to line 3 by TRANS-RECORD and line 3 is connected to line 4 and line 6. All three lines are connected to line 11 by TRANS-RECORD. Line 6 is also connected to line 14 by MESSAGE-RECORD, and both line 6 and line 14 are connected to line 8 by MESSAGE-RECORD. All three of those lines are connected to line 16 by MESSAGE-RECORD and so forth.

Figure 6.3 shows all of the connections in this code, which is highly interconnected. Figure 6.4 depicts a larger program, showing some of the connections. Any attempt to modularize the program in its existing form, as the lines in Figure 6.4 might do, for example, is likely to result

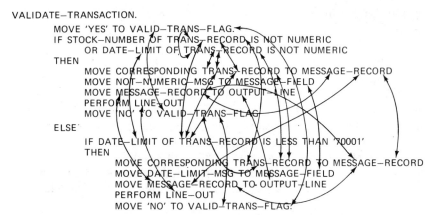

```
VALIDATE—TRANSACTION.
      MOVE 'YES' TO VALID—TRANS—FLAG.
      IF STOCK—NUMBER OF TRANS—RECORD IS NOT NUMERIC
         OR DATE—LIMIT OF TRANS—RECORD IS NOT NUMERIC
      THEN
            MOVE CORRESPONDING TRANS—RECORD TO MESSAGE—RECORD
            MOVE NOT—NUMERIC—MSG TO MESSAGE—FIELD
            MOVE MESSAGE—RECORD TO OUTPUT—LINE
            PERFORM LINE—OUT
            MOVE 'NO' TO VALID—TRANS—FLAG
      ELSE
            IF DATE—LIMIT OF TRANS—RECORD IS LESS THAN '70001'
            THEN
                  MOVE CORRESPONDING TRANS—RECORD TO MESSAGE—RECORD
                  MOVE DATE—LIMIT—MSG TO MESSAGE—FIELD
                  MOVE MESSAGE—RECORD TO OUTPUT—LINE
                  PERFORM LINE—OUT
                  MOVE 'NO' TO VALID—TRANS—FLAG.
```

Figure 6.3   Connections between lines of code.

in a high degree of connections among the pieces. One major measure of
coupling is the number of connections that cross module boundaries.
The modules in Figure 6.4 all share a large number of data elements
with the other modules. It usually is difficult or impossible to modularize existing code without producing highly coupled modules. Instead,
highly related code should be grouped together during design, when
code can be "moved around" merely by deciding to do so. Then,
divisions can be made through areas of low relationships, as in Figure
6.5. Here, for example, the number of data elements shared between the
middle module and all other modules is four.

The concept of binding essentially means grouping the highly related
elements of code together. This allows the designer to be fairly success-
ful at segmenting the highly related groups of elements into modules
that have relatively low coupling between them.

The Dimensions of Coupling

Some connection must exist among modules in a program, or else they
would not be part of the same program. The objective is to minimize the
coupling among modules. Unlike binding, which can be evaluated
basically on a single dimension, coupling has three dimensions (See
Figure 6.6). If the measure on any of the dimensions is large, then the
coupling will be high. In order to reduce coupling successfully, all
dimensions must be small. One dimension is "type of connection": the
mechanism used to connect modules. Another is "size": how big is the

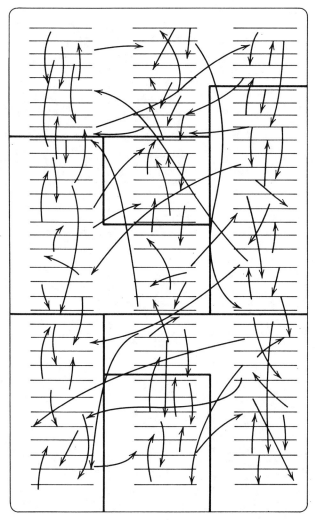

Figure 6.4 Dividing existing code.

connection? The third dimension is "what is communicated" via the connection. Each of these dimensions will be dealt with in turn. Actually, there is a fourth dimension, "clarity." The easier it is to understand the connection, the less likely another module will have to be considered in order to understand, fix, or change a given module.

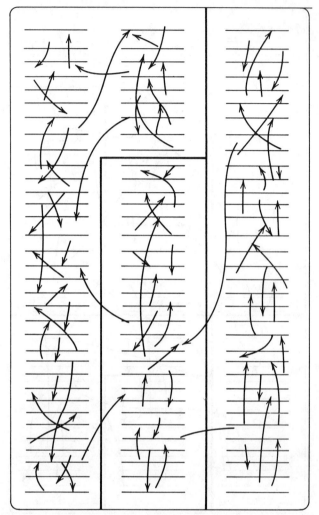

Figure 6.5   Code designed for few connections between modules.

Types of Connections

The scale of "type of connection" goes from CALL to PERFORM to "external connection", as shown in Figure 6.7. On this scale, the most complex, confusing, error-prone way to pass data from one module to another is via an external data connection. An external connection

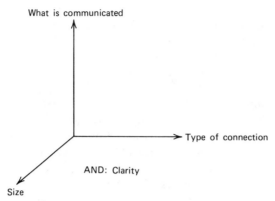

Figure 6.6 Dimensions of coupling.

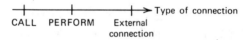

Figure 6.7 Type of connection.

exists when one module gains direct access to a data element or instruction within another module. In PL/1, this is accomplished via the EXTERNAL attribute. In assembler, a VCON is used. In order to see the difficulties caused by passing data through an external connection, consider the example shown in Figure 6.8. Here, GET A COMMAND calls READ TERMINAL to read a line of data from the terminal.

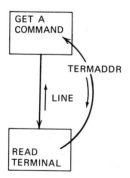

Figure 6.8 Coupling by an external variable.

Since there is only one terminal, it was (unfortunately) decided to have READ TERMINAL access the terminal address directly. The terminal address is stored within GET A COMMAND. Thus, the only parameter that needs to be passed to READ TERMINAL is for the line of data. The arrow denoting the external connection starts from *within* READ TERMINAL and goes to *within* GET A COMMAND. This is because the connection is from *inside* READ TERMINAL to *inside* GET A COMMAND.

This simple example can probably be made to work about as easily as if both data elements were passed as parameters. The difficulty comes when changes are made. If a new caller for READ TERMINAL is added to the program, such as GET A DATA LINE, as in Figure 6.9, and wishes to read from another terminal, a problem exists. GET A DATA LINE cannot pass a terminal address since READ TERMINAL will use the terminal address specified in GET A COMMAND. GET A DATA LINE must use the same external linkage to access the terminal address within GET A COMMAND. It can then put its own terminal address in the location that READ TERMINAL accesses.

Extra complexity must now be added to avoid an error in GET A COMMAND. Either GET A COMMAND must be inspected to see whether it initializes the terminal address each time—which it probably would not—or GET A DATA LINE must save the original terminal address and store it back again after the call to READ TERMINAL. Consider one characteristic of the result in either case. Should GET A DATA LINE make a mistake in saving or restoring the terminal address, it is likely that GET A COMMAND will encounter the error. Coupling via an external variable results in a situation where an error in the coding in one module causes an error to occur in a different module

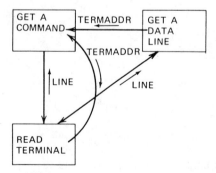

Figure 6.9   Another caller.

(i.e., a high degree of coupling). Low coupling reduces the likelihood that modules other than the one encountering the problem will have to be considered in order to fix the error.

The problem is considerably worse in an asynchronous (e.g. on-line) environment. If GET A COMMAND and GET A DATA LINE can be invoked asynchronously, then the previous mechanism of saving and restoring the terminal address does not work. If GET A DATA LINE saves the original terminal address, replaces it with its own, and is suspended prior to replacing the terminal address and then GET A COMMAND is invoked, an error will result. GET A COMMAND will read from the wrong terminal. Not only is the previous solution of saving and restoring the terminal address not sufficient, the author is aware of no mechanism *whatsoever* that can fix the problem while allowing GET A DATA LINE and GET A COMMAND to execute asynchronously. The only way to avoid an error is to ensure that GET A COMMAND cannot execute while GET A DATA LINE is suspended and vice versa. This can be accomplished by a serialization mechanism such as ENQ/DEQ or a lock word. This is an unfortunate restriction, since there is no logical reason why both modules cannot otherwise be allowed to execute asynchronously. The restriction has come only because of the choice of the external mechanism used to communicate data.

In addition, errors that result from any mistake in the use of the serialization mechanism have the worst possible characteristics. Such errors will be intermittent and will typically happen only under periods of heavy load. They will be difficult to reproduce or debug during off-line testing. Thus, any change seems to fix the problem. Once the system is in production, though, usually during some peak period, it will again come crashing down.

In summary, the problems with connecting modules via external variables are as follows:

- Connections of this type proliferate to every new caller, since each is required to make use of the same mechanism in order to communicate to the called module.
- It is difficult, at best, to have the modules work correctly in an asynchronous environment.
- Errors require simultaneous consideration of all modules involved. In an asynchronous environment, these errors are intermittent and typically happen only during periods of heavy load.

- The interface is not obvious. That is, it is not necessarily clear from the call statement that two parameters are being passed instead of the explicitly declared single parameter, LINE.

Lower on the scale of "type of connection" is the PERFORM statement. The difference between the CALL and the PERFORM statements relative to type of connection is primarily one of clarity. It is much easier to understand a sequence of code that includes the statement CALL AVERAGE USING DOLLARS 1, DOLLARS 2, AVG. DOLLARS than it is to understand the same sequence of instructions that included instead the statement PERFORM AVG. Lack of clarity is, however, not the worst problem with using PERFORM statements to link modules. The major problem with implementing modules as paragraphs will be studied relative to the dimension of size.

Because it avoids the problems with the previous forms of coupling, the simplest, easiest to understand, least error-prone of the three mechanisms for passing data from one module to another is the CALL statement. It also works in an asynchronous environment.

Size of Connections

A second dimension of coupling is "size" (see Figure 6.10). The less data passed in the interface, the lower the coupling.

Although size almost speaks for itself, there are some subtleties involved. How *much* data is passed through the interface is not the issue. Rather, it is the amount of data passed *each time* the interface is used. Also, when gauging the amount of data, it is the number of distinct data items to be understood that causes the coupling to increase. A simple method of gauging the amount of data is to count the number of parameters. Note, however, that the coupling is not reduced by assembling all of the data into a structure that is passed as a single parameter. This would reduce the clarity while still passing the same amount of data. Thus it would be more likely that the code that generates the structure would have to be inspected in order for one to

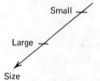

Small

Large

Size   ***Figure 6.10***   The dimension of size.

understand the structure or to check that it was assembled properly. It is more generally true that, with a given number of data items being passed, the *maximum* number of names provides the minimum amount of coupling, because it leads to the best understandability. An exception is that groups of *related* data items do not need to have separate names for each item. For example, an array of hours worked for each day in the month is most easily understood and handled as a single array. The same is true with externally defined records. They are usually simpler to pass as single parameters (see "Passing Fields Versus Records" in Chapter 7). But when arrays of unrelated items are built arbitrarily they become harder to understand.

In summary, although some data must be passed across an interface, the less data there is, the lower the coupling. Typically, interfaces can be reduced to two to four parameters. Also, the clearer the names for the data that is passed, the lower the coupling.

Before leaving this dimension of coupling, it may be useful to examine a widely used technique that results in high coupling owing to the size of the interface: passing data items through a shared data area. In COBOL, the entire linkage section is often shared with all called modules. Also, a data division copy-member, such as the master-record definition, which is copied into all modules, constitutes a shared data area. In PL/1, either of these or the include/external statements can be used to generate a shared data area. If modules are implemented as paragraphs, the data division is a shared data area. In FORTRAN, there is a formal mechanism for generating a shared data area known as COMMON. In assembler, shared data areas are often known as control blocks.

To examine the effects of a shared data area on complexity, consider the example illustrated in Figure 6.11. Here, a data area is shared by six modules. Consider the size of the coupling in this situation. The first element of data in the shared data area connects module A to module B. B is also connected to A, since either can affect the other by any error in their use of that data element. Also, A is connected to C and C to A, and so are A and D, A and E, and A and F. There are also connections between B and C, B and D, B and E, and B and F; and between C and D, C and E, and C and F, and so forth. The number of connections that results from the first element of data in the shared data area is 30, as is illustrated in Figure 6.12. An equal number of connections results from the second element of data, and so on. In fact, the number of resulting connections is so high that it is easier to calculate than to count. The number of connections is equal to $M\times(M-1)\times N$, where M is the

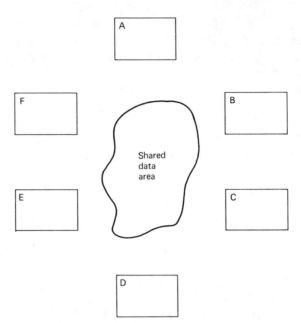

Figure 6.11   Common coupling.

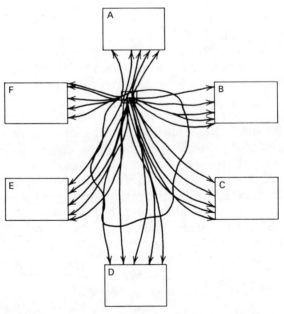

Figure 6.12   Coupling from a single shared element.

number of modules and N is the number of elements in the shared data area. For this example, assuming a rather modest 25 variables in the shared data area, the number of connections is 750 (6 $\times$ 5 $\times$ 25). Notice that the number of connections increases as the square of the number of modules involved.

It might be questioned whether it is relevant to count all of these connections. In particular, it may seem that those connections for data items not used within a particular module should not be counted (even though they *are* defined there).

Unfortunately, these are the connections most likely to cause difficulty. In Figure 6.12 assume B does not use the first data item and consider expanding the size of the first data item without recompiling module B. If B uses any data items in the shared data area, there is bound to be a problem because B will no longer have the correct offset for its data items. Furthermore, this problem does not really result from an error in the coding of B. It results from a much more obscure incompatibility between the definition of the shared data area in multiple modules. If B stores into its data items, it will probably cause errors in modules other than B (and other than those using the first data element). In fact, it is very likely that B will not be the one to encounter an error, even though it is, strictly speaking, the module with the error.

Thus, it is typically necessary to recompile all modules whenever the definition of the shared data area is changed. But even so, changes to the shared data area can still cause errors if all modules are not considered. Assume that a data item is added, which again is not used by B, but which has the same name as a local loop variable used within B. Now, a recompile of B without consideration of the code inside again causes an error (unless the compiler can catch it). Although, strictly speaking, the problem is in B, the error may again occur in a different module. Thus, it is precisely those connections which are *not* being intentionally used on which errors can unsuspectingly propagate! In fact, the ones being used intentionally will typically cause the fewest problems.

The worst problem with a shared data area, though, is that it results in exactly the same difficulty that occurred with external connections. It is difficult to have two or more modules successfully call a third when the parameters must be passed through a single location in memory. Even in a static batch environment, it is hard to coordinate saving and restoring data in the shared data area. In an environment where the modules can be invoked asynchronously, it again becomes necessary to incorporate a serialization mechanism. Also, any errors encountered will typically be intermittent, only happen under load, and require simultaneous consideration of all modules involved in order to find and fix the problem.

Sometimes the problem is further compounded by the following logic: "In order to provide maximum flexibility, put *all* variables into. the shared data area. Then, any module can access any data item it might need." But in practice, shared data areas are changed only if absolutely necessary. This strong reluctance to make changes results from experience: it has been difficult to get everything working again when changes have been made to similar shared areas in the past. Adding more variables to the common area makes it *more* difficult to make changes, not easier. But being difficult to change is the *opposite* of being flexible!

If a common area is already present in an existing system or is required by the environment, the number of connections (and thus the complexity) can be drastically reduced by segmenting the shared data area as in Figure 6.13. Define a different segment for the variables shared by each group of modules. In FORTRAN, this can be implemented via NAMED COMMON. In assembler, separate control

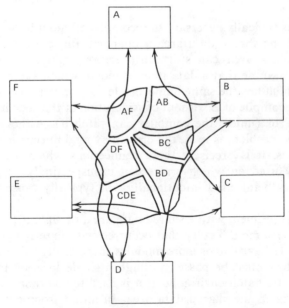

Figure 6.13   The shared area segmented.

blocks can be assigned. In the case of modules sharing a common terminal work area (as in an on-line system), give each module its own segment(s) of the work area. In this way, changes to any one module do not affect other modules' use of the common area for their variables. However, in no case should parameters be passed through the common area.

This difficulty with common data areas does not imply that control blocks should not be used. For example, they are valuable, for saving the status of I/O devices or other resources. The difficulties arise when they are used to pass data between functions. More specifically, problems arise when more than one module stores into and/or accesses the data. Control blocks that are accessed by only one module (which returns the status from within the control blocks to callers that need it) do not cause the difficulties described here.

What Is Communicated

A third dimension of Coupling is "what is communicated" (Figure 6.14). Two things can be communicated, control or data. The most complex type of communication is Hybrid Coupling. This is when one module modifies the code of another. The term "hybrid" is used because the code being modified is data to the module modifying it, but control to the module being modified. Luckily this technique is not possible in most languages (other than assembler).

While this technique is seldom used today because of the complexity it causes, it is useful to examine the reason for the complexity. Any errors made by the module that *modifies* the code typically result in problems within the module *being* modified. Thus the module that encounters the error is not the one that must be changed in order to fix the error. Worst of all, problems are extremely difficult to debug, since

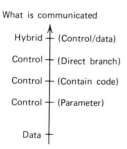

Figure 6.14 What is communicated.

what is in memory does not match the source listing and since it is extremely difficult to find what module(s) modify the code, even through automated means.

Another way in which control can be shared between two modules is when one module branches directly to a point inside another module. The connection is to instructions that affect the control of both modules. This connection is possible in assembler and also possible when paragraphs are used as modules. The difficulty here is that changes cannot accurately be made to the module being branched into without first assessing the impact on the location(s) that branch into it. These location(s) are difficult to find, and it is next to impossible to determine whether all occurrences have been found. If, as is possible in assembler, the branch is to an unlabeled statement (via an offset from a labeled one), the mere existence of such a branch may not even be suspected. Here again, multiple segments of code must be considered in order to make a change to a single one.

A module can also affect the control of another module if it is contained within the flow of the second module. This can be done in assembler, via any mechanism allowing multiple entry points, or in COBOL (if paragraphs are used as modules), using the PERFORM THROUGH statement. The statement PERFORM A THROUGH B causes A THROUGH B to be treated as a module in exactly the same form as would paragraph C in the statement PERFORM C. If paragraph C lies between paragraphs A and B, an unexpected change will occur in the module A THROUGH B when any change is made to the module C. Moreover, it may not be obvious that paragraph C is included within another module. Although still error prone, this situation results in lower coupling than the previous ones since it is less prone to errors and a little easier to identify.

The clearest and least error-prone way that control can be passed from one module to another is to pass elements of control as arguments. But even this is unnecessarily complex, as will be discussed next.

In the example in Figure 6.15, the module GET MMDDYY OR JULIAN DATE returns the date in the format determined by TYPE-SWITCH. (Often such a module is called GET DATE, but, as explained in the discussion of module names in Chapter 5, this is not an accurate representation of its actual function). Note that the OR in the module name implies a nonfunctionally bound module. This is consistent with the existence of the parameter TYPESWITCH, because if the module had only one function, there would be no need to pass it a switch to tell it which function to perform.

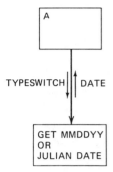

Figure 6.15   Control coupling.

An alternative structure (Figure 6.16) eliminates the switch. While the example here is a simple one, the direction of the difference is significant, even though the difference is slight. The solution in Figure 6.16 is slightly *easier* to code than the one in Figure 6.15. The code in GET JULIAN DATE and GET MMDDYY is also contained in the date routine in Figure 6.15. However, the code necessary to test the switch in Figure 6.15 has been eliminated. In the module A, where it previously set TYPESWITCH to JULIAN and called to get a date, it now simply calls GET JULIAN DATE. Where it set the switch to get MMDDYY dates, then called to get a date, it now calls GET MMDDYY. Thus, A is also slightly simpler because it does not need to set the switch. The result is also slightly easier to understand, because when reading the module A, the code CALL GET JULIAN DATE is clearer than the previous SET TYPESWITCH TO 1; CALL GET MMDDYY OR JULIAN DATE. There is less likelihood of having to

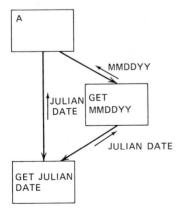

Figure 6.16   A simpler solution.

inspect the module GET MMDDYY OR JULIAN DATE to see how it uses TYPESWITCH and what its different settings are. In addition, there is less likelihood of remembering incorrectly and making an error. Notice that in the first example, the switch was used to keep track of whether the julian date needed to be translated into MMDDYY format. In the second example, this information is inherent in the structure. GET JULIAN DATE will return to either caller. If its caller was GET MMDDYY, it is because the translation is to be done. It is unnecessary for the programmer to write logic to keep track of what is being done.

With such a simple example, either solution probably can be made to work fairly easily. The significance is that the solution that eliminates the switch is slightly *easier* to implement, understand, and use. The author is, however, aware of a date routine that did cause actual problems because of the control coupling involved. (This routine returned many different formats of date—admittedly via hybrid coupling instead of a switch.)

The simplest type of communication is when data is passed. It can be proved, with information theory, that data coupling is sufficient for any program. Thus, control coupling in any form always involves extra, unnecessary communication and coupling. Control coupling also directly involves one module in the control of another. This compromises the objective of being able to consider each module as separately as possible.

The way to stay low on this scale of "what is communicated" is to pass only data as parameters. But sometimes it can be difficult to distinguish between program switches and data. Some binary parameters are not program switches—for example, male/female indicators. Conversely, many program switches are not binary—for example, a multistate return code that the caller must analyze in order to determine the appropriate error-recovery action to be taken. To determine whether a particular parameter is a program switch or not, look at the parameter from the point of view of the module that sets it. If the parameter is being set in order to tell another module what to do, then it is a program switch (since it involves one module in the control of another). Note that errors can result either if the module getting the switch does not perform the appropriate action, or if the module that sets the switch sets it incorrectly. Debugging may require examination of both modules.

Referring back to Figure 6.15, for example, the module A clearly is affected by what the date module does in response to TYPESWITCH.

Thus, this is a program switch. On the other hand, a module whose function is to validate something passed to it and that returns a parameter called VALID is not affected by what the caller does with the data. Thus, the programmer need not be concerned with what the caller will do with the VALID parameter while writing the validate module. The caller may use the item, print it on an error report, or discard it—all entirely irrelevant to the coding of the validate module.

In practice, it is not crucial to be able to determine accurately the difference between a program switch and a data parameter that indicates status. The point is that program switches can be eliminated. If the designer discovers what seems to be program switch and cannot find an alternative that eliminates it, there is little value in having identified it as a program switch. Conversely, deciding that a parameter is data does not mean that it cannot be eliminated. Thus, the identification of parameters as program switches is primarily to indicate where time might be profitably spent looking for improvements.

The objective is to minimize all dimensions present in any connection. The simplest connections are those which use a <u>CALL</u> to pass a <u>small</u> number of <u>data</u> parameters in the clearest way possible. See Figure 6.17. By only designing structures of separately compiled programs with single entry points, all that will remain is to eliminate program switches and to reduce the number of data parameters.

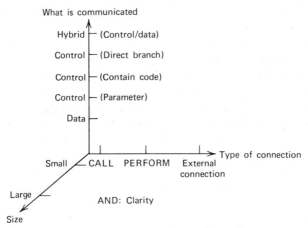

Figure 6.17 Dimensions of coupling.

Summary

Coupling measures the strength of relationships between modules. The lower the coupling, the less likely that other modules have to be considered in order to understand, fix, or change a given module. Coupling primarily comes from connections: two modules referencing the same data item or instruction. The fewer data items referenced by two segments of code, the lower the coupling.

Segments of code tend to share many data items with other segments unless they are specifically designed otherwise. Attempts to modularize existing code typically result in highly coupled segments being physically separated, which increases complexity and maintenance time. The same thing can happen if programs are modularized without sufficient attention being paid to producing functional modules that pass a small number of parameters. It is important to organize the code *before* it is written so that highly related things can be grouped together into independent, functional modules.

In order to achieve low coupling, it is necessary to deal with four considerations: the mechanism used to connect the two modules; how big the connection is; what is being communicated via the connection; and the clarity of the interface.

The types of connections include CALL, PERFORM, and external connections. An external connection exists when one module accesses a location within another module. Even if one module uses this technique to pass data to another module, it will not be very easy to follow or understand what is happening. As soon as there are more callers for the same module, though, it is difficult to coordinate the use of the single location to pass data to the called module. An error made by any of the callers can cause other callers to execute incorrectly. Thus there is a high degree of dependence among all callers. In an on-line environment, there is *no* way to coordinate the use of the single data area other than by forcing the callers to run serially, which is complex, error prone, and degrades response time. Errors made in this environment are usually intermittent, time-dependent, and often occur only under load. These are the hardest kinds of problems to find and fix.

Use of the PERFORM statement as a type of connection also forces all callers to share a single location for data parameters. Thus, again, the errors in one caller can cause other callers to execute incorrectly. Although the PERFORM statement is slightly more visible than the external connection, there is still no clear definition of what data items are shared. The CALL statement is the simplest, most flexible, most visible, and most versatile of the linkage mechanisms in most high level languages.

Relative to the size of a connection, the less data passed, the lower the coupling. When gauging the amount of data, it is the number of distinct data items to be understood that causes the coupling to increase. Arrays of data or externally defined records can be passed and considered as single data items. Also, the easier it is to understand what is being passed, the less likely the module that passes the data will have to be inspected to determine what the data is. Thus it is valuable to assign and pass each distinct data item as a separate parameter.

One approach resulting in *high* coupling because of the size of the connection is when modules reference a common data area. This can be done in PL/1 by the external attribute, in FORTRAN via COMMON; in assembler, common data areas are often called control blocks. Another way to create this situation is to copy the field definition of an external record into all modules. The number of connections resulting from this technique is enormous. The number increases as the square of the number of modules. For a relatively modest example of six modules sharing twenty-five data elements, the number of connections in 750. The modules are highly interdependent, and there are many ways in which modules can end up executing improperly because of errors made in other modules.

Passing data via common data areas also results in the same problems that occur relative to external connections. There is a single location for modules to use when calling any given module. Thus, there is a coordination problem in the static environment. In an asynchronous environment, callers must be serialized. Errors are time-dependent, intermittent, and typically occur only under load. Fixing these errors requires simultaneous consideration of all modules involved. There is usually a strong reluctance to change the definition of the shared data area because of the complexity involved in trying to get all of the code working again. Thus, this technique does not contribute to independence of modules, changeability, or flexibility.

Modules can share control and/or data. There are several ways to share control which vary in resulting complexity. However, sharing control is not necessary and complicates both modules sharing the control. Data coupling is necessary and sufficient for implementing computer programs. Functional modules do not need to tell each other what to do by sharing control.

7

Techniques and Tips

The purpose of this chapter is to provide tips and techniques that can help the designer perform structured design faster and more easily. The rules of structured design have been dealt with in previous chapters. Any technique that achieves a high degree of independence among the pieces of a program (i.e., low coupling) can be used. This chapter presents some approaches and techniques for improving coupling and binding. A technique for generating initial structure charts will be covered in a later chapter. Regardless of the technique used to generate an initial chart, though it is always appropriate to look for possible improvements.

Binding and coupling are sufficient to govern the modularization of programs. Using *only* binding and coupling, however, would be like learning carpentry by reading the building codes manual. It might be possible, but it would probably take the beginning carpenter a long time to pick up the techniques that allow high-quality houses to be built rapidly. This chapter does not provide rules that *must* be followed but rather offers techniques, tips, and hints that may save the reader the necessity of discovering these things by trial and error. The purpose here is not to be precise and rigorous but rather to be helpful and useful.

Improving structure charts is similar to climbing a hill. The hill to be climbed is a simple one; that is, there are no hidden valleys or local high places. In other words, there is one top which can be reached from anywhere on the hill by always walking up hill. The route taken is not critical. As long as each step takes us higher up the hill, we will eventually reach the top. In structured design terms, any change that improves coupling and/or binding is an improvement. By making a series of improvements to binding and/or coupling, progress is made through better and better structures until no further possibilities for improvements can be seen. The order in which the improvements are made is basically arbitrary.

DESIGN APPROACH

This section includes concepts and techniques that are relevant before you starting to use structured design, and when doing an initial chart.

The Overall Approach

The approach of structured design is to build programs as structures of single-function, separately-compiled, well-named modules that are data-coupled by as few parameters as possible. This one sentence encompasses all of the concepts dealt with in previous chapters.

First, start with a structure that meets the specifications and use binding and coupling concepts to evaluate step-by-step improvements. In this manner, making improvements that progressively move the structure to the top of the "hill" (the most independence) is a straightforward process.

Ideally, having the initial structure meet all of the specifications would make the resulting process straightforward. In actual practice, though, it is sometimes not practical to meet *all* of the specifications in the initial structure, nor is it necessary. Sometimes it is difficult to make the initial structure meet every single specification. It turns out to be quite workable, when necessary, to keep aside specifications that were difficult to implement in the initial structure until later in the process. As improvements are made in the structure, it becomes easier and easier to make changes because of the increasing independence, for example, and integrate the withheld specifications—since they are, essentially, changes. In order to integrate the specifications into the structure, it is likely that additional parameters and/or functions may need to be added. While this would not seem to be an "improvement" to the chart, binding and coupling are not the ways to evaluate the addition of specifications. The point is to not consume an inordinate amount of time trying to make the initial structure meet every single specification. In actual practice, specifications can be added to the chart as improvements are made, as long as it is realized that extra parameters and/or complexity may have to be added in order to do so.

Define the Required Parameters

Identify all of the parameters necessary to make the structure meet the specifications. This is an essential part of the process of structured design. The primary goal is high module independence. Parameters are the most direct measure of the amount of independence achieved. Many different functional breakdowns can usually be made for any program. The amount of communication needed between modules can usually be seen only through the process of specifying the parameters necessary to make the structure meet the specifications. Thus, deciding what parameters are needed typically will highlight any difficulties with the structure. It is the parameters that usually enable evaluation of alternative functional structures relative to the goal of highly independent modules.

Work with the Complete Structure Chart

It is suggested that those doing structured design always work with the entire structure chart for any given program.

If the size of the program necessitates two designers, it is advantageous for both designers to work together on the entire structure chart. Few programs are so large that one or two designers cannot design the entire structure chart. "Program" means all of the code that can execute as a result of an execute card in the job control language, in other words, one job step. In an on-line system, the equivalent concept is a transaction: the application code that can execute as a result of a transaction entering the system. The problems with dividing a structure chart and having different people work on different portions of it are that improvements may involve either of the following:

1. Moving modules from one portion of the structure to another, or

2. Identifying functions that are common to different parts of the structure.

These kinds of improvements may be missed if the design is divided up between designers.

On the other hand, programs *are* written that are, in fact, too large for a single designer to design in any reasonable amount of time. Examples of programs in this category are operating systems, compilers, sort routines, and so forth. But compilers and sort routines are often divided into phases. When this is the case, it is practical to have a different designer work on each phase. It is interesting to note that such phases typically are purely data-coupled and highly functional within themselves. That is, each phase leaves only data for the next phase, and all of any particular function is accomplished within a given phase.

In some cases, however, it may be necessary to have different designers work on different parts of the same structure. In these cases, the success of the structuring effort will be dependent upon the degree of communication between the designers. The more the designers communicate, the greater the likelihood of finding common functions and of being able to identify modules that should move from one designer's portion of the structure to another.

Standard Forms

One of the most useful hints that could possibly be given is to indicate what the final solution will look like. It turns out that this *can* be done, in a general way at least. Figure 7.1 indicates the structure common to

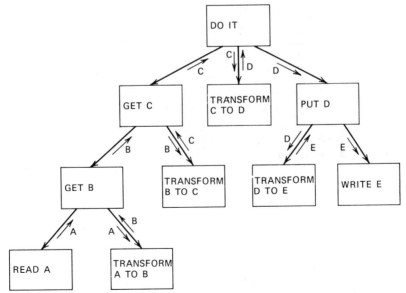

Figure 7.1   Common structure for input/process/output types of programs.

most business applications: they typically get data from somewhere (I/O or memory), transform the data in some manner, and put the data somewhere (to I/O or memory). This characteristic would *not* be true, for example, of a program that calculated the trajectory of a satellite around the earth. However, the structure pictured in Figure 7.1 and its variations will be appropriate for almost all of the programs with the characteristic indicated.

Note some characteristics of this structure. Data is read by a module at the bottom of the structure. As the data is moved upwards in the structure, it is refined farther and farther (i.e., edited, validated, and/or selected, etc.). Then, any major transformation of the data occurs under control of the top module. The resulting data is passed downwards to be prepared (e.g., formatted, converted, combined, and/or totalled, etc.) as appropriate for output such as printing.

Notice that the structure contains modules that transform data—for example TRANSFORM A TO B—but are independent of where the data comes from or where the results are sent. These are the ones most likely to be useful for later programs. It is at least as easy to write a function that is independent of the source of the data as it is to write it dependent on the source of the data. The former way though results in a code that is reusable, replaceable, and independent of the rest of the program. Thus it can be designed, developed, fixed, changed, replaced and reused independent of the rest of the code. There are also modules that basically pass data to the transform modules and check to ensure that the process is proceeding without error, for example GET B.

Variations on this structure include having multiple modules that return streams of data to the top module or to other modules in the structure. Multiple modules can dispose of streams of data. Multiple transforms can be called by any module, and transforms may call other transforms. Modules such as those on the left leg in Figure 7.1 may produce output such as error messages. Modules such as those on the right may read data such as that necessary to determine execution-time formatting. It is important to realize that this structure does *not* imply that all input should be on the left, all processing in the middle, and all output on the right. To do so would be to group functions because they are all input or processing or output; this would be logical binding. Similarly, it does not imply initialize on the left, process in the middle, and terminate on the right, which would also result in logical binding.

One of the most common variations on this structure is the absence of a transform called from the top module. Most business applications do not have a major transformation of the data, but merely select, edit, and format the data.

The business-type programs that do not result in this structure usually result in the one shown in Figure 7.2. The transaction structure will process transactions it receives from above (as in Figure 7.2) or from below. The salient characteristic of this structure is that there is a multiway decision to call any one of a number of modules, each of which processes a particular type of transaction. These transaction modules may very possibly call other modules, some of which may also be called by other transaction modules.

The transaction structure is appropriate independent of the number of transactions to be handled. It is not necessary to add extra levels simply to reduce the number of calls from the top module. The transactions referred to can be transactions such as in an on-line system, but they can also be any set of items where it is appropriate to take various specific actions based on the type of item. An example of this would be multiple-transaction types into a master-file update program. The transaction structure can be the top of a structure for a program or may occur as one of the modules in the previous common structure, typically within a leg like the one on the left in Figure 7.1.

Match the Program Structure to the Real World

A significant suggestion for rapidly arriving at functional, changeable structures is to design the same relationships among modules as exist among the functions in the real world. Take, for example, a requirement to retrieve data from a remote sensing device. The device is connected through an auto-answer mechanism to a telephone hookup that can be

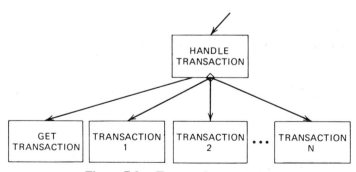

Figure 7.2   Transaction structure.

dialed by the computer. In this case, the remote sensing unit immediately sends its data whenever a call comes through. Figure 7.3 shows two possible structures for implementing this requirement. Either structure will work. In design A, however, consider the following: In the real world, is receiving a part of dialing? Since receiving is not part of dialing in the real world, it is more appropriate to choose design B, where DIAL and RECEIVE are both called by a function probably named MAKE A CALL or GET THE DATA.

Since design A *can* be made to work, it may be useful to examine why design B is preferable. The advantage is that reasonable changes tend to impact design B less than they do design A. Consider what happens if a new type of remote sensing terminal is added to the network. The new terminal may require a character to be transmitted to it before it will send its data. The DIAL module in design A could not be used to dial the line for the new terminal. If modified for the new terminal, it cannot be used for the old terminal. If modified to accommodate both, the coupling increases in order for dial to be told whether or not to transmit a character first. In design B, all that is necessary is to add a module that transmits characters.

The same conclusion can be reached by considering binding or coupling. The DIAL module in design A should have been named DIAL AND RECEIVE, which then indicates the nonfunctional binding. Further, the coupling between DIAL and its caller must include the data being received, which is stronger coupling to the DIAL module than in

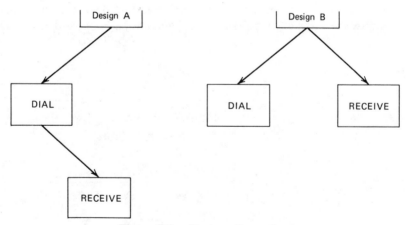

Figure 7.3   Design alternatives.

design B. Making the structure of the program match the structure of the problem in the real world allows the designer to achieve high binding and low coupling more rapidly. It is especially useful when generating an initial chart. It also serves as a good check to spot possible binding and coupling problems not previously identified.

Another example of matching the program structure to the structure of the problem in the real world could be the necessity of designing reports for five departments within a company. Initially these reports are all to be the same. The question is, should there be five modules, one for each department, or should there be one report module for all five departments? If the reports involved are complicated enough to consume more than about one page of code, then the modules being referred to will be the top modules. All modules below these top modules will probably be common, whether the one- or the five-module solution is chosen.

In order to evaluate whether the one- or the five-module solution is appropriate, evaluate the relationship among the reports in the real world. If the departments are all independent and coincidentally want the same report format and content today, but may want different contents and/or formats tomorrow, then the solution should be implemented as five separate and distinctly named modules. Note that the generation of all but the first of the five modules is a trivial renaming process once the first module is coded and working. If, on the other hand, the reports are required by upper-level management and must have the same data and format, not only now but in the event of a change, then the one-module solution is appropriate.

What if the one-module solution is chosen by mistake when, in fact, the five-module situation exists? The designer should then convert to the other solution when the first change occurs that impacts only a specific report. In other words, once it is identified that reports can change independently, independent modules should be made to facilitate those independent changes. This is preferable to attempting to modify one module to accomplish the independent requirements of multiple different reports or functions. Admittedly, it will be tempting to modify the module when the first change comes along rather than implementing multiple modules at that time. Similarly, it will be tempting to do the same when the second independent change occurs. By the time the independent modifications become difficult to make, it is already too late to make modules independent easily. Thus, it is important to do it while it is trivial—before implementing the first independent change.

When the program structure matches the problem structure, single changes in the problem have the best chance of being implemented as single changes in the program. Otherwise, each change in the problem could cause multiple changes in the program.

Err on the Side of Dividing Too Far Initially

Early in the design process, if there is a question as to whether to divide a given module farther or not, divide it. It is much better at this point to err on the side of dividing into too many modules rather than too few. This will facilitate identifying common modules. It is easy to merge modules back into their callers later in the design phase if it is still appropriate at that point.

Do not, however, create extra *modules* in an effort to have the structure chart exhibit all that the program does. The structure chart alone will never be sufficient to exhibit all of the program specifications: module specifications are needed. The rest of this chapter presents much more important reasons for creating and for not creating modules than just for improving the descriptiveness of the structure chart.

GENERAL DESIGN GUIDELINES

This section presents concepts and guidelines that are generally useful throughout the structured design process itself.

The Major Guidelines

The major guidelines of structured design and independence, simplicity, and observability. The goal is to have the best of all three. Independence is primary because it is the mechanism used to reduce the complexity. As was discussed in Chapter 3, the complexity of programs grows faster than their size. The purpose of structured design is to approach as closely as possible the condition of having the complexity be simply proportional to the size, for example to have a 500-line program be only as complex as 10 50-line relatively independently. The independence achieved through appropriate modularization reduces the complexity, achieve the simplifications.

Simplicity is not the same as writing the fewest lines of code. For example, to make a module highly independent of its environment, it is very desirable that it check its parameters to see if they are reasonable prior to, for example, trying to take the square root. It may also be true that the callers check to see that they are not passing negative numbers to SQUARE ROOT before calling it. While this does not constitute the minimum amount of code, it does increase the independence. Minimum lines of code and simplicity are ultimately conflicting objectives anyway. The fewest lines of code can probably be arrived at only through a process of optimization. This is by definition not the simplest way to write the code and usually results in code that is hard to change.

Observability measures how easy it is to see why a program does what it does. While a simpler program is easier to understand and, thus, more observable, observability is basically a dimension different from independence and simplicity. Observability is enhanced, for example, by clear meaningful names for programs and parameters and by a good prologue describing the function of the module and how it uses its parameters.

Elements of a Functional Module

The following are possible elements of a functional module. First, any module must certainly do its assigned job. Second, if there is any circumstance in which the module is going to be unable to do its assigned job, it must be able to indicate this to its caller. Typically, this is done through a parameter such as ERROR. Further, if the module returns a stream of data to its caller, then an essential part of that function is the ability to indicate to its caller when there is no more data, namely, EOF.

A module should do error recovery relevant to accomplishing its function. To require callers to do the error recovery makes each caller highly related to the called module. The error recovery will also be repeated multiple times within a program if there is more than one caller, either now or later. Coupling is usually increased, since multiple-state return codes are often needed to identify error types so the callers can take appropriate error recovery. This is an example of how misplaced function increases coupling.

A module should issue error messages that are dependent upon the particular status of errors encountered. If, however, the error message is dependent only upon the yes/no status of the error parameter which indicates that the module cannot do its job, then typically the error message is more useful and more descriptive when issued from the immediate caller. Notice that since the error parameter passes from the module to its caller anyway, the choice of whether to issue the error message from the caller or the called program cannot be evaluated on the basis of coupling.

The last potential element of any function is to produce reports and/or logs of actions taken. Whenever the specifications for a program require that details about the internal function of a module be reported or otherwise logged, the simplest solution is to have the module that performs the detailed action produce the report or log the item. Any attempt to report or log details about actions taken by one module from some other module will increase the coupling. This is because it will be necessary to pass the detailed results as parameters between the modules. In other words, coupling is lowest when the details are reported from the module in which the details are already known.

There may be a tendency in the above type of situation to give the module involved what seems to be a nonfunctional name, such as DO THE FUNCTION AND LOG IT. Consider a module whose function is to update fields in a master file record. Versions of this record before and after the update are to be written to a log file. The WRITE TO LOG module should be invoked directly from the module doing the updating. The tendency may be to give it a name such as UPDATE MASTER RECORD AND LOG THE RESULTS TO THE LOG FILE. By the rules in the chapter on binding, the AND indicates nonfunctional binding. The purpose of this list of possible elements of a function is to identify those elements which are *implicitly* part of any function, if the specifications so require. In other words, it is neither necessary nor productive to explicitly include these parts of the function in the module's name. Thus, UPDATE MASTER FILE RECORD is an adequate name for the update module, whether or not the specifications require the results to be written to a log file.

The primary purpose of high binding is to achieve low coupling. In the update module example above, the lowest coupling is achieved by having the update module log or report the details of its own actions. It is counterproductive to argue that the binding is not functional and should be improved. Even the binding cannot be improved, since any attempt to produce the report or log from another module will cause *that* module to be even less functionally bound. It is simplest to name modules without trying to include explicitly any of the elements listed here.

Black-Box Characteristics

Another useful characteristic of functional modules is to have them be like a black box. A *black box* refers to something whose insides cannot be viewed. A module is like a black box when it can be properly used without one's needing to inspect the code inside to see how it accomplishes its function. A radio is an everyday example of an item with this characteristic: it is not necessary for the user to understand the electronics and circuitry inside a radio in order to make proper use of it. The dials and nobs are like parameters and can be used to make the radio perform its function without an understanding of the inside. In fact, radios are implemented internally in a multitude of different ways while still performing the same basic functions.

Black-box-like modules execute the same way independent of what module calls them. Modules whose code is dependent on a specific caller are prone to errors if new modules call them. Their code probably must be inspected in order for them to be used properly.

Black box characteristics make modules more independent of their environment, although such characteristics do not relate directly to either binding or coupling. Anything that can be done to make a module more easily usable enhances this characteristic of being like a black box. For example easily understood, well-named parameters help the usability of a module. A good prologue that indicates how the parameters are used and the function the module performs can also enhance its usability. Note that not having to inspect the code inside the module means not having to look at *executable* code. Certainly, the prologue can and should be looked at by the user or caller of a module.

Avoid Duplicating Functions

One of the major benefits of structured design is that functions do not need to be implemented within the same program more than once. Monolithic programs tend to duplicate functions whenever there are different data areas to which a function is to be applied.

There are several problems with having the same function implemented more than once within the same program. One is that time is wasted writing (and debugging) the function multiple times instead of only once. Also, the functions will typically be implemented slightly differently for each occurrence. Thus, the functions may not be consistent in all cases. But the worst problem is when changes are to be made.

All of the occurrences of the function have to be changed, and the changes must be compatible with one another. It is usually difficult to identify the existence of multiple functions and to know *where* they exist. Moreover, the functions usually have been implemented at least slightly differently, possibly even by different people. Not only does it take extra time to figure out how to change each (different) occurrence, but unusual combinations of data can often be processed slightly differently by the various implementations. This necessitates yet new changes.

During the design process it may be noticed that two modules seem quite similar to one another but are not quite the same (as in the example in Figure 7.4). If so, try to identify the common portion of the two modules and define that as a separate module, as in Figure 7.5. Several variations can occur. F1, or F2, or both can be empty or small enough to be merged into their caller(s). Thus, the result may be one, two, or three modules, depending on the situation.

Sometimes a two-step procedure for eliminating a duplicate function is easier to see, especially when the similarity seems to be small pieces of function. The first step is to eliminate the actual duplication by passing a parameter from one place to the other. For example, assume two places both test the same data for the same condition. Have one place test the data for the condition and pass a resulting status parameter to the other location. This eliminates the need to implement any change in the test in multiple places, which makes changes easier. The second step is to search for alternatives that improve the coupling resulting from the added parameter. This is a unique case in which adding a parameter is actually an *improvement*, because it eliminates duplicate function(s). It also defines a much more visible item, which is easier to work to eliminate than the more obscure duplication of function. Typically the parameter will eventually be eliminated anyway as the duplicate func-

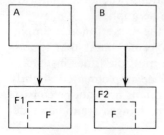

Figure 7.4   Similar modules.

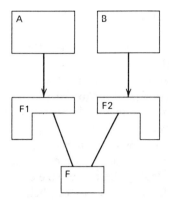

Figure 7.5 Duplicate function eliminated.

tions are moved closer and closer together, finally ending up within the same module. These later moves will often be justified on the basis of eliminating the parameter that was added in the first step.

Implement Each Specification in Only One Module

Implementing each part of the specifications in only one module—or in as few modules as possible—is similar to implementing each function in only one module. This way, if the specification changes, only one module needs to be changed. Consider the example in Figure 7.6. This

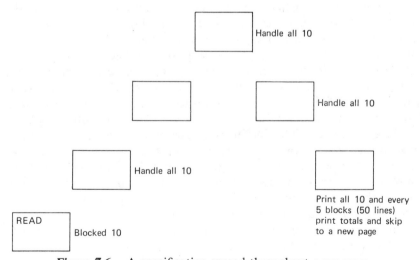

Figure 7.6 A specification spread throughout a program.

program, which was probably written some years ago, accesses blocks of 10 records rather than individual records. The program is not shown as a structure because it was probably a monolithic program. The READ portion reads in a block of 10 records. Since they are all in memory, the next function handles all 10. Further along, another thing is done to all 10, and again something else is done to all 10. Finally, each of the 10 records is printed and, after every fifth block (which makes 50 lines), totals are printed and a skip is made to a new page.

Although the program works, problems arise when a new type of disk drive is introduced and recommendations are made to increase the block size to 15. Although the process of increasing the buffer size and each of the loops to handle the fifteen records per block is straightforward, as often as not one or more of the functions that have been handling all 10 records is missed. The result is that some function does not occur on the last 5 records in each block of 15. There is also a difficulty in the print routine. The complexity here is substantial, since every fifth block is no longer the signal to print totals and skip to a new page. In fact, it can take several tries to perfect the algorithm for skipping to a new page.

The problem is that dependence on a particular external specification, such as the blocking factor, has found its way into many parts of the code. As a result, simple changes in specifications, such as a change in block size from ten to fifteen, are more difficult to implement than is necessary.

Implementing each part of the specifications in only one module could be accomplished for this example in the following fashion. Have a READ module read the block and pass only one of the records to the rest of the program. Each part of the program that needed to loop for 10 records is now slightly simpler, since the loop can be eliminated. The print portion simply prints each record as it arrives and after every fiftieth record prints the totals and skips to a new page. Implementing a change in block size from 10 to 15 requires a change in only one place, the READ module. The buffer is increased for 15 records, and a physical read is done each fifteenth record instead of every tenth. Now the rest of the program will operate correctly. It is impossible for the rest of the program *not* to operate correctly. It gets the same sequence of data in the same form as before. The correct operation is assured without even having to inspect any of the rest of the program.

Further, if *all* programs in the installation that read this file use the same READ module, then this trivial change to the READ module is sufficient to make them all work with the new blocking factor. It really could have been basically that easy to change blocking factors as new disk technology was introduced. It all comes from implementing a single specification in a single module. It also comes from being willing to implement even simple modules if they can constitute a single place where a possible change can be made, instead of choosing solutions where a single change in a specification requires changes in multiple places.

Opt for Changeability

Another way to evaluate alternative structures is to see which of them is impacted less by reasonable changes. Since one of the primary objectives of structured design is to make it easier to make changes (both to fix an error and implement a new requirement), this is an important measure. In evaluating alternative structures, the one that is less impacted by a reasonable change is an improvement over one in which the same change would be harder to make—assuming all other things are equal, such as the binding and coupling.

Looking at the impact of reasonable changes is also a useful way to check a design. Consider a set of new or changed requirements that might reasonably be expected to occur. Include especially those which are highly likely to occur. See if the changes can be accommodated with simple modifications to the current structure. The objectives of binding and coupling are to produce structures that can be easily changed. Thus, if it is difficult to accommodate likely changes, there are usually problems within the structure, typically binding and coupling problems not previously noticed. Eliminating these binding and coupling problems may also point the way toward additional improvements. Thus, considering reasonable changes becomes a good test of the quality of the design, regardless of whether the changes are eventually made or not.

Binding, Coupling, and Changeability Are Complementary

Since there are three measures suggested above, it may be asked what should be done if one alternative improves one measure but one or both of the other measures are made worse. The answer is, don't make the change. Improvements are only those changes which improve one or more measures *without* causing a worsening in another measure. Typically, one measure is improved without a noticeable change in the others. (When looking back it can often be seen that the other measures have actually improved, but that may not be obvious when the change is first made.) Changes in which one measure improves and others are made worse are usually combinations of several individual changes, some of which are improvements and some of which are not. It is the *combination* that results in one measure improving while another measure is made worse. The problem can be avoided by evaluating the individual changes. The ones that improve the structure are justified and the ones that cause measurements to get worse are not justified.

Choose the Simplest Solution

Choose the simplest solution to the immediate problem. This suggestion may seem superfluous, since the statement says essentially that the simplest solution to the immediate problem is the simplest solution to the immediate problem. The value lies in observing the typical results of efforts made to improve generality. Often upon first encountering a need for a table-handling routine, there is a temptation to write a *general* table-handling routine. This, it may be thought, will benefit future efforts, but two problems arise.

First, the attempt to provide generality to a routine typically results in added parameters. But flexibility and reusability are usually achieved through *fewer* parameters, not more. This is because the modules most likely to be used in the future are those which are simple, well defined, and easy to use. These characteristics are enhanced by having *fewer* parameters, not more. "ERROR and EOF Parameters," below, gives an example of this.

Second, experience shows that, as often as not, the added generality does not turn out to be what is needed. Thus, parameters may be added that complicate the original implementation *and* the future implementation, while not providing the generality needed! Consider the perplexity of the maintenance programmer for the original module trying to determine the reason for the unnecessary parameter. A good understanding of the parameter indicates that it is not needed, which is confusing, because certainly a parameter would not have been added unnecessarily.

Finally, in all cases, any extra effort necessary to produce a more general routine is charged to the wrong project. It is always easier to implement the simple, straightforward approach than the general one. Thus, the scope of the original project is unnecessarily expanded in an attempt to accommodate unknown and imprecise future requirements, which may or may not materialize. And it usually takes less total time to implement a specific solution first and then modify that solution to the general case. Thus, the two-step solution not only will result in applying the proper effort to the proper project, but may also be the most efficient way to get the general routine working anyway.

Another situation may occur during implementation. An oversight during design may result in the need for a change to the structure. Based on what has already been coded, the simplest solution may be to pass a program switch. During design, other options may have been able to eliminate the program switch, but these require reworking existing modules now. If the simplest solution to the current problem is a program switch, then implement it that way. In other words, if the simplest solution to fixing design oversights is nonfunctional in some way but is still the simplest solution, then that is the option to choose.

By the same token, it is probably not productive to delay or compromise the design of individual programs within a system of programs in an effort to identify modules that will be common across programs in the system. Attempts to do so will require a large amount of communication between the designers. The complexity rises very sharply as efforts are made to optimize the design of the whole system simultaneously. Worst of all, it is difficult to get a final decision on any particular program. The design efforts can lengthen substantially.

Each program in a system should be modularized relatively independently. Define modules based on the requirements of the program being designed. Whatever knowledge the designer has of the rest of the programs in the system will, of course, aid in identifying modules that may be usable later and changes that are likely to occur. Make descriptions of the specifications for designed modules available to other designers. Then they can decide if they can use modules that have already been designed.

Allow for Flexibility

Flexibility is the ability to adapt to new requirements not currently specified for the program. Versatility is the range of functions a program can perform. Simple solutions are easier to modify, which enhances flexibility. It is tempting to try to provide flexibility for expected future needs by writing more versatile code. But trying to satisfy assumed future needs today increases the complexity and implementation time of the current solution and often does not provide the function that turns out to be needed in the future either. The increased complexity makes it harder to change the program, which *decreases* the flexibility. Typically, the unfortunate result is that the extra time spent ends up *decreasing* the flexibility!

It is impossible to code in *all* of the functions that will be needed by the program in the future. Also, future needs are often the most ill defined and the most difficult to get agreement and approval on. Because of this, they are often among the hardest and most costly parts of the current program to implement. This compounds the disadvantages of attempting to implement them now rather than later. And the justification and funding for the current project seldom include *any* allowance for implementing future needs anyway.

Flexibility is also enhanced by *allowing* for all possibilities, rather than designing a solution specific to today's particular situation. Assume that today's specifications may change. Choose the alternatives that will be least affected if changes do occur.

An example of allowing for flexibility rather than providing for it now might be the building of a road. Assume it is known that additional interchanges must later be added to a road that must be built now. Trying to guess where the interchanges will be and building them now will probably result in more total work rather than less. Not only will all the interchanges still have to be built at some point, but time spent building ones that turn out to be in the wrong spot will be wasted. They may even have to be dug up. Instead, allow for interchanges to be built later by, for example, not building stone walls down the side of the road. Number the intersections by the mileage along the road rather than sequentially numbering each interchange. This choice makes it simpler to add new interchanges in the future.

In a similar vein, race cars are not built that turn only to the left (on the assumption that racing will *always* be done in a counterclockwise direction). When a house is built, functions are provided that are versatile and independent. Sometimes when water is drawn, it is desirable to have a hot stove burner available immediately to heat the water. However, to assume that this will *always* be the case and to provide a connection between the water and stove functions such that the burner automatically turns on when water is drawn *limits* the flexibility instead of enhancing the function. Yet these kinds of connections are often implemented in computer programs in an effort to make them "easier to use."

One data-processing development group produced a good payroll system but then spent some more time writing code to make the payroll system run itself. Input was processed on the right day, paychecks were cut automatically just prior to payday, and registers were reproduced on the first and the fifteenth. Everything was great until the first time the fifteenth fell on a Sunday. (Production was not run on Sunday.) Monday was the sixteenth and the registers would not run on the sixteenth. In fact, there was no way to *get* the registers to run on the sixteenth. Then a power failure left the computers down on the day paychecks were usually cut. The next day was the wrong day and there was no way to get the system to produce paychecks. The development group ended up writing even *more* code to circumvent the code they had written previously. This is an example of how designing solutions that assume things will always be as they are today often results in decreased rather than increased flexibility.

Calls Across Levels

Structured design specifically allows and in fact encourages calls across levels, as shown in Figure 7.7. There is no need for all modules at a given level to be of equivalent "importance." On the contrary, once a function is defined and available as a separate module, it should be invoked from

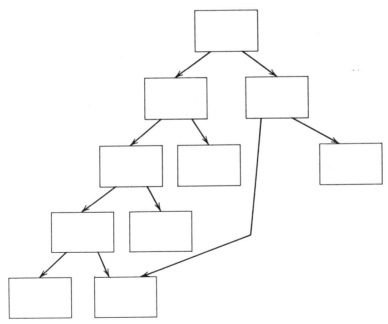

Figure 7.7 A call across levels.

wherever it is needed within the program. For examples such as SQUARE ROOT or WRITE TO LOG, it should be obvious that there should be no restrictions on the number or choice of levels from which the modules can be called. There is no reason to restrict any other modules either. Thus, calls across levels are specifically allowed and encouraged.

Calls *up* across levels, as in Figure 7.8, are also allowed. The value is precisely the same as before, and for good reason. Figure 7.8 depicts the exact same structure as Figure 7.7. It is merely drawn differently.

Figure 7.9 depicts a possible problem with calling across levels. The problem does not relate to structured design but, rather, *may* be a language restriction, depending on the language. Here, module A calls B, which calls C, which calls A again. Unless the language specifically allows for recursion, for example via re-entrant coding, the return point for the original call to A will be lost. Thus, when A tries to return to its original caller, it will return instead to module C, typically resulting in an endless loop. APL specifically allows recursion. Of course, the logic

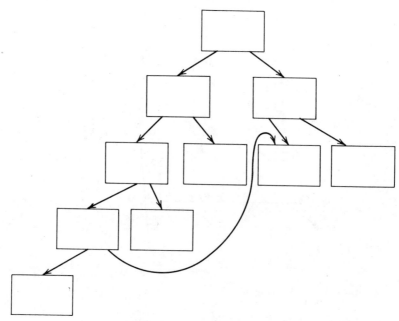

Figure 7.8   A call across levels.

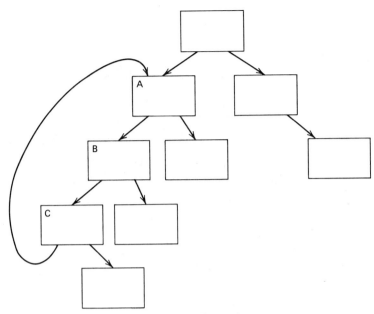

Figure 7.9   Recursion.

must be proper in order to allow any recursive calls to exit from the implied loop eventually.

Recursion will seldom happen unintentionally, but it *can* happen unintentionally in surprisingly straightforward circumstances. Consider a WRITE ERROR MESSAGE module that calls WRITE TO TERMINAL. If WRITE TO TERMINAL encounters an error, it may seem desirable to call WRITE ERROR MESSAGE. This results in a need for recursion—and some code to avoid an endless loop.

Thus, the only problem to check for when calling across levels is recursion, *if* the language does not allow for it. There are, however, some simple ways of checking for possible recursion. If the structure chart *can* be drawn in such a way that all calls are downwards (whether or not it is, in fact, drawn this way), then there is no recursion. If calls that go *up* across levels call only modules that call no others, then there cannot be recursion. Or if calls up across levels are to modules that only call other modules which themselves contain no calls, as in Figure 7.10, there can be no recursion. These checks allow the designer to rapidly evaluate that there can be no possibility of recursion for most structure

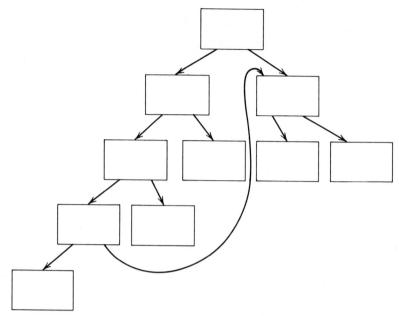

Figure 7.10   No recursion.

charts. The few structure charts that do not satisfy these criteria need to be checked in more depth for recursion if the language does not allow for it.

ERROR Parameters Are Unique to Each Interface

Most modules need the ability to return a parameter such as ERROR to their callers in order to indicate if they are unable to do their function. Even though the parameter may appear in multiple interfaces, it means a different thing for each interface. In each case, it is a signal from a module only to its immediate caller that the called module was unable to perform its function.

In Figure 7.11 an ERROR parameter from READ TAPE to READ FILE means only that READ TAPE cannot do its function. The ERROR parameter should almost always be binary. Here, it indicates that the tape can be read, or that it cannot be. All possible error recovery has already been attempted by READ TAPE before it returns to its caller. The caller can call READ TAPE again if it is desirable for READ TAPE to attempt its error recovery an additional time. Whether

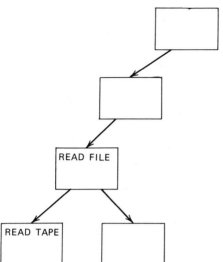

Figure 7.11   Error parameters have different meanings at different levels.

or not an ERROR from READ TAPE causes READ FILE to return an error to its caller also is dependent on the particular specification of READ FILE. For example, READ FILE may take alternative actions such as requesting that a backup file be made available. If, and only if, READ FILE determines that it cannot complete its function, will it return ERROR to *its* caller. The same happens above it in the structure. Even seemingly "fatal" errors may not result in the top module going to end-of-job. Unknown to all modules below, the top module may ask the operator whether a second pass should be made on a new tape, for example.

As an aside, a point can be made relative to Structured Programming. If Figure 7.11 is turned 90 degrees counterclockwise, a figure similar to those resulting from segmentation in structured programming is achieved. In fact, if the structured programming segments are implemented as modules, the figures are equivalent. It has been argued that a GO-TO should be allowed if a fatal error is encountered deep within the structure, in order to branch immediately to end-of-job. This, the argument goes, prevents the need for checking upon return from each invoked segment whether to continue processing or to return immediately to the next higher invoking segment because of an error. But if segments are made highly independent and functional, several things result. The mechanism for returning to the next higher level in case of errors will be included anyway as part of the functional requirements of the segment. Moreover, determining end-of-job conditions is not functionally related to lower level segments such as READ TAPE. READ TAPE does not have the data necessary to determine whether the error is, in fact, fatal—neither does READ FILE, nor any other segment in between! Only the top segment knows whether, for example, the program is to do another pass before going to end-of-job. Segments in between may also have error recovery. Thus, the question about the need for unconditional branches to end-of-job from invoked segments is an unnecessary one in functional low-coupled structures.

ERROR and EOF Parameters

ERROR and EOF (end-of-file) parameters are often required elements of status needing to be passed between modules in a structure. Nonetheless, as with any other parameter, if alternatives can be found that eliminate either of these in any particular case, the coupling will be improved. Consider the following two examples relative to the ERROR parameter.

One is a module whose function is to return descriptions for three-letter ID's. The description is printed on a report. If a description is not available, the line on the report should include the three-letter ID. It might seem than an error parameter should be returned in case a code was passed for which there was no description.

In this case, the need for the error parameter can be eliminated by having the module always return a string of text. If the description is available, the string of text returned is the description. If there is no description in the table for the ID, then the ID itself is returned as the string of text. This approach eliminates the need not only for the called module to set an ERROR parameter but also for the caller to check the error parameter and construct the text itself.

Secondly, consider a module that validates that a password is correct for a given user-ID. The password and the user-ID are passed to the module, which returns a valid-switch saying whether or not the password is correct. (The valid-switch is equivalent to an error parameter.) By moving a small piece of function into the caller, the valid-switch can be eliminated. Instead of having VALIDATE check whether the password is correct (after looking up the correct password), have the caller do that check. Simply pass down the user-ID. VALIDATE PASSWORD then returns the valid password. The same result is achieved, but now VALIDATE PASSWORD works with only *two* parameters, having eliminated the valid-switch. The password is now a *return* parameter instead of an input parameter.

The new module is no longer VALIDATE PASSWORD, but rather GET VALID PASSWORD. Notice that it is more useful than VALIDATE PASSWORD. It can be used not only to validate, but to get the password when needed. Notice also that the usability of the module increased as the number of parameters *decreased*. Further, since it can be used for both needs, the case never arises where VALIDATE PASSWORD rejects passwords returned by GET VALID PASSWORD. This could happen if passwords were stored in special formats that had to be translated by the modules and if changes were made to the two modules that were not exactly consistent.

It is not unusual for the usability of a module to increase as the number of parameters decreases. The decreased coupling makes the module more functional and more independent of its environment and thus more usable elsewhere. As was indicated above in "Choose the Simplest Solution," the temptation when attempting to make a module more flexible is to parameterize it—that is, to *increase* the number of parameters in an attempt to increase its function. More commonly, as in this case, flexibility increases as the number of parameters is *decreased*.

Initialization Parameters

Initialization parameters can usually be avoided. An initialization parameter is a switch that tells a module to initialize itself. Not only does an initialization parameter complicate the interface for every caller, but it involves some other module in the function of the module that gets the initialization parameter. Thus the usability goes down. The module requires an environment where there is some other module that will initialize it.

Modules that do not need to be initialized are simpler to use. If some initialization is required, it is simpler if the module initializes itself upon the first entry. One way to accomplish this is for the module to have a "first-time" switch within it. However, this is not always the only solution. Consider a READ module that opens its file the first time it is called. If the module is in assembler, it can interrogate the I/O block to see if the file is open, rather than opening the file based on a first-time switch. Alternately, if the I/O routine has a return code that indicates an unopened file when a read is attempted, then the module could use this as the signal to open the file. Assuming that it also closes the file when it reads end-of-file, it could, if desired, be called again after the file was closed. It would reopen the file and begin to read through it again. This is somewhat more flexible and usable than one which would only read through the file once due to a first-time switch.

In some cases, the environment may make an initialization parameter unavoidable. If so, at least implement it in such a way that it compromises the functionality of as few *other* modules as possible. For example, a second entry point used to initialize such a module can reduce the coupling for all other callers since they would not have to define an initialization parameter. In addition, initialize all the modules that need it from one INITIALIZATION module. Such a module will, of course, have temporal binding. But *any* module that initializes another one is going to have temporal binding. At least only one module is temporally bound, rather than many modules being temporally bound and highly interrelated as they all initialize each other. Further, make the initialization module a separate module that is called by the top module. The top module then becomes slightly temporally bound but is not as complicated and as related to the other modules in the structure as it would be if it *contained* all of the initialization code. Also, use lots of comments. There should be comments in the initialization module indicating what modules it is initializing. There should be comments in the modules being initialized that they will not work without being initialized by some other module. Make it as clear as possible what is happening so that, although the functionality must suffer, observability does not have to be compromised as well.

READ, WRITE ERROR, and PRINT Modules

The reader may wonder if READ, WRITE ERROR, and PRINT modules really need to exist as separately compiled modules, especially in high-level languages. The answer is yes. One reason is that even though the modules are small, it is unproductive to code them again and again. A module that includes a read, write, or print function and the necessary logic to open and close the file can be used easily by any other program needing to read the same file. Also, its source can be modified slightly to adapt it to a new file. More important, the READ, WRITE ERROR, and PRINT modules serve as a single point to which modifications can be made that affect the entire program or set of programs that use the module. For a READ module, fairly surprising things can be done very simply. If the I/O routine does not deblock, the READ module can deblock the records (resulting in the kinds of benefits referred to above in "Implement Each Specification in. Only One Module"). Modifying an existing record to add an extra field can be handled with ease. Simply modify the READ module to compress the extra field out again and all the old programs will work with the new file. Any new programs needing the new field use a new read routine that does not compress the field out. As old programs are converted to use the new field, they simply call the new READ module. The input file can even be split onto multiple physical files! The READ module simply gathers the pieces together, reformats them in the old form, and returns that.

A WRITE ERROR module is a single place where changes can be made having to do with the output device. The error messages could be reformatted to go on an output line of a different size. They could be sent to both a video and a hard-copy device or to a storage file. With the addition of a severity parameter, errors of different severities could be counted and reported at the end of a program. All of these changes can be made in the single WRITE ERROR module rather than from the multiple places where errors are written.

If the operating system does not have a spooling capability, a PRINT module is an excellent place to implement, or allow for later implementation of, such a capability. The PRINT module could be passed a printer number and a line to be printed. One file is printed directly and other files are written to temporary storage devices. When the stream of data being physically printed signals end-of-file, one of the other files is read back and physically printed. Like the WRITE ERROR module, the output could be reformatted, redirected, or duplicated all by simple changes within the PRINT module.

The READ FILE-X module is easier to use if it opens the file itself and closes it on EOF. That way, all a caller has to do is call to get records. The WRITE FILE-Y module is easier to use if it automatically opens the file and closes it upon receiving EOF from a caller. If the file is open for update (read/write), have READ FILE-Z open the file and WRITE FILE-Z close it. Once each of these four types of modules has been written for the first file, it can be used by all programs which access that file. This avoids writing the same logic more than once per file. Modules for other files can be created easily by using the source of the first file's modules as prototypes. Thus, these four modules need to be written only once.

Why is the operating system's read routine not sufficient to serve as the READ module? The main reason is that it does not supply an automatic open on the first read (or close on EOF). Also, some of the changes desirable for the READ module require recoding. It is impractical to expect to modify the operating system's I/O routines in order to shield the program from any physical changes in the file, such as adding a field or breaking up the record. Although these kinds of changes are, admittedly, seldom made to files, it is not because the need is never there. Rather, it has been nearly impossible to modify files this way without causing severe errors and maintenance problems for most programs. So the reluctance to change files in these ways is understandable. With routines as described above maybe data processing can now be more responsive to the users' need for changes to be done accurately and quickly.

A WRITE ERROR Module

One technique commonly used for implementing a WRITE ERROR function is shown on the left in Figure 7.12. The caller passes an error number to WRITE ERROR, which looks up the message in a table and writes it. Contrast that to a WRITE ERROR module that is passed the text of the error message, as on the right in Figure 7.12. The latter one is usually preferable. This is because passing an error number involves the WRITE ERROR module in the function of all the modules that call it. For example, any change to the calling module that affects an error message will require two modules to be modified instead of one, the caller and the WRITE ERROR module. It is also harder for the maintenance programmer to understand the calling module, because the text describing its errors is in the WRITE ERROR module rather than right beside the code that detects the error.

Sometimes the error number implementation is chosen, on the assumption that it makes changing error messages easier, since they are all in one place. However, this implementation does not increase flexibility, it *decreases* it. Once an error message is put into the table for one caller, it becomes very difficult ever to consider rewording it because it is nearly impossible to know what other modules may now use the same error message. Thus, the original caller loses ownership of its own error

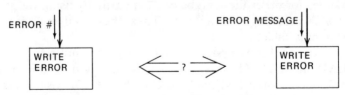

Figure 7.12   Alternatives for writing error messages.

message. Too often the unfortunate result is that the error message is not changed, even though it may have been found to be ambiguous or misleading. In this case, the lack of flexibility affects the user direct-ly.

Another tendency is for new modules to use error messages already in the table rather than adding their own unique ones to the table. In fact, this is another reason why the error number implementation is often chosen: so that multiple callers can use the same error message without having to store it more than once. In fact, the only real advantage of the error number implementation is to save memory (and at the cost of flexibility). But even the need to issue the same error message from multiple places is questionable. While it *might* make sense if functions were repeated multiple times within a program, functional structures should not need to issue the same error message from more than one place. To issue the same message from two distinct functions can only cause the error message to be ambiguous, since the user would not be able to tell which function detected the error. For example, it might be tempting to have a compiler issue the message "syntax error" from multiple places as different points of syntax were checked. But it would be much more helpful at least to indicate, via distinct error messages, what kind of syntax checking was being done in each case.

Even in the unusual case where the same message is to be issued from two different places within the program, it would be more flexible to have two copies of the error message, one within each module. Then, if one caller wishes to change the text of the error message differently from the other, it can be done easily.

Thus, having the error message text with the code that detects the error makes the message easier to check, understand, and change. When anything affecting error messages is considered, the message is beside the code that detects the error, rather than in another module. Thus, passing the error message text to the WRITE ERROR module is preferable to passing an error number.

There is at least one situation, though, in which the error number implementation *would* be preferable. This is when a program must support multiple languages interchangeably, in other words, the error messages must be presented in a language appropriate to the location where the program is being run. Because of the additional specifica-tions, flexibility is enhanced by having all error messages contained within the same module. Then only one module needs to be replaced in order to effect a language change. In order to avoid the problems discussed above, though, there should be no attempt to use the same error message from multiple places. Even where memory is so critical that this kind of memory saving might be worth the complexity it would cause, there are other alternatives that save memory but produce less complexity. The error messages could be eliminated entirely by issuing the error number and requiring the user to look it up in a book. This alternative, poor as it may be, is still preferable to burdening the user with error messages that are ambiguous because they are issued from multiple places (and this alternative would save a lot more memory).

IMPROVING STRUCTURE CHARTS

This section presents specific techniques that can be used to improve a structure chart once an initial chart has been developed that meets the specifications. Experience with these techniques can also help the designer build better initial charts in the future.

Eliminate Program Switches

Program switches are elements of control passed from one module to another in order for the sending module to affect the control of the receiving module. Program switches can be passed up from a called program to its caller, or down from the caller to the called program. In either case, the sending module gets involved in the function of the receiving module.

Program switches should be distinguished from parameters that merely reflect status. All binary parameters are not program switches. For example, a male/female indicator is binary but certainly is not a program switch. Also, ERROR, EOF, and parameters such as VALID-FLAG are usually status indicators. A parameter is a status indicator if the module setting the parameter is not affected by what the receiving module does with it—it merely indicates status. For example, a READ module is not affected by what a caller does on EOF. Conversely, the top module in Figure 6.15 is quite dependent on whether the date switch it passes to GET DATE is interpreted correctly.

Conversely, program switches do not all have to be binary. In fact, multiple-state error parameters are usually program switches rather than status codes. This is because what is usually happening is that the caller is being required to do the error recovery for the module returning the multiple-state error code. That is why the multiple-state switch is being returned to the caller.

Program switches passed *downwards* usually indicate that the called module contains multiple functions. The functions can often be identified by considering the actions taken by the called module in response to each value of the program switch. For example, a GET DATE module that is passed a TYPE OF FORMAT parameter actually converts date into any one of several formats based on the parameter. Each of these is a separate function and should be in separately callable modules.

Program switches that are passed *upwards* typically indicate misplaced function. Typically, they are passed upwards to enable code higher in the structure to be conditionally executed, based on the outcome of conditions tested below it in the structure. In Figure 7.13, for example, if an error message is to be written based on errors detected when editing cards, then a program switch will have to be passed from GET RECORD to COMPUTE PAY in order to effect this conditional call to PUT ERROR MESSAGE.

To eliminate program switches that are passed upwards in the structure, move the conditional code down, move the testing of the condition up in the structure, or move both so that they meet in the middle. A solution for Figure 7.13 is to call PUT ERROR MESSAGE from EDIT CARD, thus moving the conditional call downward in the structure. (COMPUTE PAY may still need to call PUT ERROR MESSAGE for errors it detects.) In this particular case, GET RECORD also needs to know whether or not the card was in error, in

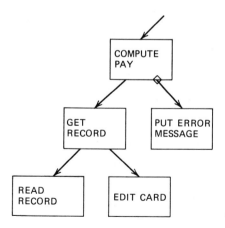

Figure 7.13   A need for a switch.

order to determine whether to get another record before returning to COMPUTE PAY. Thus, as was said earlier in this chapter, if the error message to be put simply indicates that the card was or was not in error (as opposed to detailed information as to what the error was), it can be preferable to call PUT ERROR MESSAGE from GET RECORD.

There is always an alternative that eliminates a program switch. This is not to say that the designer can always find the alternative, nor does it imply that data parameters cannot also be eliminated. What it does say is that, when a designer has identified a parameter as a program switch, it is worth some time to attempt to find an alternative that eliminates the program switch. Some methods have been indicated here for eliminating switches, depending on whether they are being passed down or up in the structure.

Extracting a Module from Its Caller

Some tests for pulling a module out of its caller follow. These can be used to evaluate whether or not a module called by another module should remain separate or be merged back into its caller.

1   Is it functional? For a module to remain as a separate module it must be functional. Check to see if it satisfies the requirements of functionality as covered in Chapter 5. In other words, is there a simple phrase that completely describes its function without the use of multiple verbs, phrases, or otherwise implying more than one thing?

2   Does it have low coupling? In order to remain a separate module, it must both be functional and have low coupling. Low coupling means that it must not be control-coupled and that the number of parameters should not be excessive.

Just because a module is functional and low coupled does not mean that it should stay a module. It must also satisfy at least one alternative of the following requirement:

3a Is it usable elsewhere (now or later)? If the module is called from two modules within the same structure, then this requirement is satisfied. This requirement is also satisfied if, in the designer's opinion, it is likely, or even possible, that the module could be called from some place else in the same program or in another program in the future.

3b Does it simplify an overly complex caller? An overly complex caller is one that either is longer than one listing page of executable code (15 to 30 lines if APL) or, in the designer's opinion, is too complex to be handled, understood, and changed easily. However, not all modules called from a complex caller necessarily simplify their caller. In order to simplify the caller, a called module must remove a significant portion of lines of code and/or it must remove some branching logic, in other words, at least one conditional IF statement removed (as opposed to duplicated).

The distinction between removing and duplicating some branching logic can be illustrated by an example. Consider a test to see if a total is greater than, equal to, or less than zero. It could physically be extracated as a separate module. As a separate module, it can be given a functional name—TEST TOTAL. It would be low coupled: it needs the total as an input parameter and the high-low-equal status as a return parameter. Assuming the caller was large and/or complex enough, it could be argued that it should remain a module because it simplifies the caller by removing some branching logic. However, the calling module *still* needs to test the return status for high, low, or equal. The IF statement in the caller is merely duplicated, rather than being actually removed. Thus, it does not simplify the caller.

A module should be kept if it is functional, has low coupling, and is either usable elsewhere now or later or simplifies a caller that is too big or complex.

Actually, these are requirements all modules should satisfy. But using the test early in the design phase may suggest merging modules into their callers that later end up having multiple callers. That is why this test is best applied toward the end of the design.

Although these are tests for pulling a module out of its caller, they can also be used toward the end of the design to see if a module should remain a module. Assume that the module has been merged into its caller and use the tests to see if pulling it out again would be justified. If it is justified, then the module should be retained. If not, the module should be merged into its caller.

The Presence or Absence of a Call Does Not Affect Coupling

Coupling is reduced when a module can be made to work with fewer parameters. Coupling is not affected by how *many* callers a module has. In fact, the more functional and lower-coupled a module is, the more likely it is to have many callers. These points are of particular relevance when looking at an overall structure chart. The count of the number of parameters in the complete structure chart is not a valid measure of coupling. The coupling is not a property of the structure, but rather is a property of the interface to any given module. Using the count of the total number of parameters in the structure as the measure of coupling will lead the designer in the wrong direction in some cases. Specifically, it implies that the *fewer* callers a module has, the better the coupling. In fact, using this measure, the coupling improves every time a module is merged into its caller. Following this logic, all modules would eventually be compressed into their callers, until the single monolithic solution is reached. The fallacy here is that the objective is not to eliminate *all* the parameters. The objective is to divide programs into multiple, relatively independent pieces, each of which will inevitably have parameters that couple it to the rest of the program. Low coupling is achieved by reducing the number of parameters any given module has in its interface. In other words, the interface to a given module counts only once, independent of how many callers it has.

The creation or elimination of the additional interface is not an issue when deciding to create or delete a module. The creation or deletion of a module is done on the basis of the tests above for pulling a module out of its caller. Those tests do involve coupling. However, the fact that parameters are *totally* eliminated when a module is merged into its caller is irrelevant with regard to that test.

Module Size

The size of a module is not its governing characteristic, but it should be considered once all other objectives of structured design have been satisfied. The size of modules is a characteristic that should be considered toward the end of the design effort. The objective of structured design is to divide programs into pieces that can be handled easily and independently. Psychologists have found that an 8½-by-11-inch sheet of paper contains about the amount of information people can deal with comfortably at one time. In other words, one listing page of executable code is a size that can usually be handled easily as a unit. There are cases for modules both bigger and smaller than a page of code. But since modules that need to deviate from about one page of code are more the exception than the rule, it is well to examine each occurrence of this kind of module to see if there is, in fact, justification for the deviation in the size.

Modules Longer than One to Two Pages

Modules longer than one to two pages of executable code (or, if APL, 15 to 30 lines) should be checked to see if they can be broken down farther. Look for multiple functions or subfunctions usable, or potentially usable, elsewhere. Use the test for extracting a module from its caller (above). Do not, however, compromise functionality just to make a module smaller. If a large module truly contains only one function and contains no subfunctions usable elsewhere, then leave it as one module.

One characteristic typically true of large *functional* modules is that they usually contain little and/or simple logic, specifically, conditional branching instructions. For example, a module may either contain, or totally be, a CASE structure with multiple conditions. Even though the paragraphs of the different cases may be short, there may be so many conditions that the CASE construct constitutes more than one to two pages of executable code. Typically, a CASE construct is either a function or part of a larger function. It is unlikely for a CASE should ever be divided between two or more modules.

This is not to imply that CASE statements can never invoke other modules. The paragraphs for the different conditions can invoke other modules. But attempts to make the module smaller by grouping some conditions in one module and other conditions in another module only results in splitting a single function across two separate modules.

Modules with Less than One to Five Lines

Modules with less than one to five lines of executable code should be examined to see if there is a possible problem. Again, this is a step that should be done toward the end of the design. Previously, it was suggested that when dividing, the designer should err on the side of dividing too far, because it is always easy to merge modules back into their caller toward the end of the design. So toward the end of the design, examine modules with less than one to five lines of executable code to see if they should be merged into their callers. Use the tests above for extracting a module. Check to make sure the module is functional and low coupled. Then if the module in question is called from more than one place or seems likely to be called from another place in the future, it should be kept regardless of its size. Or if it removes even a small function from an already large or complicated caller, it should be kept. Note that even though a module may have originally been extracted in order to simplify its caller, changes during the design may have simplified the caller. Thus, toward the end of the design, it is appropriate to check to see if the caller still needs the simplification of the module in question being removed.

There is no size that is, by definition, too small for a module to be. Depending on the situation, a case can be made even for a "null" module—a module which contains no executable lines of code (except for those needed to return to the caller). In fact, a real occurrence can be cited where such a module was found to be useful. The module was requested by a physicist who was having a program written and run by a service bureau. It was a transform module that received parameters X and Y and returned them to the caller, as in Figure 7.14. The programmer noticed that the contents of the module were null; that is, X and Y were returned to the caller exactly as they came in. So, in a benevolent moment, the programmer eliminated all of the calls to the transform module so that the execution time (which was being billed) would be slightly reduced.

When the testing was completed, the physicist brought a second transform module to replace the first one. The second one was, as you might guess, not null. At this point, the programmer had to go back to all of the modules that had previously called the transform module and modify them back again to include the calls once more. The fallacy here was assuming that just because a module did a trivial job, it was not needed. In this case the module served as a place in which a single change could be made to affect multiple locations within the program.

The purpose of the preceding example is to show that no size can arbitrarily be said to be too small for a module to be. Notice that the tips included above relative to small modules would have warned against eliminating the transform module in Figure 7.14, since it was called from more than one place.

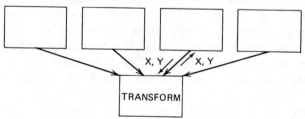

Figure 7.14   A useful "null" module.

Modules Called by More than Three to Five Others

An item worth checking into is modules called by more than three to five others (Figure 7.15). There are examples where this is quite valid, such as SQUARE ROOT, WRITE ERROR MESSAGE, or any type of utility module. For other than utility modules, however, it is unusual for a module to be called by more than three to five others.

Modules called by more than three to five others may contain two or more functions with different callers using different ones of the contained functions. If this seems to be the case, try to divide the module horizontally into two or more modules, each with a single function and only the callers that want that function (Figure 7.16). Any contained function needed by all callers may be appropriate as a separate module like the bottom one in Figure 7.16.

Figure 7.15 A module called by more than three to five others.

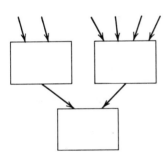

Figure 7.16 A possible solution if binding problem.

Modules that Call More than Three to Five Others

Similarly, modules that call more than three to five others, as in Figure 7.17, should be checked for the existence of possible problems. Here again, there are examples where this situation is perfectly proper, as in the transaction structure (See "Standard Forms," earlier in this chapter). More often, multiple calls from a module indicate a tendency

Figure 7.17 A module calls more than
than three to five others.

toward too much control within a single module. As in the previous
section, the problem may be a missing level. The function and control
contained within the original module may need to be divided, as in
Figure 7.18.

Calling Sequences

One situation that sometimes comes up during the design process is two
or more modules called in the same sequence from multiple places, as in
Figure 7.19. It seems desirable in those cases to create a new module to
handle that sequence of calls for the multiple callers. This is especially
true when each of the callers has the same logic around the call

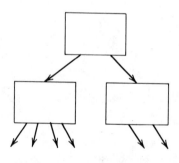

Figure 7.18 A possible solution if missing
level.

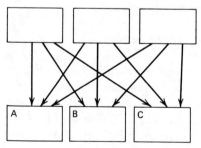

Figure 7.19 Modules called in the same
sequence from multiple places.

sequences. This logic, for example, might include conditional or iterative calls based on the status of the return parameters.

No difficulty seems to be caused by implementing a module such as D in Figure 7.20 if at least some kind of functional name can be identified for D. There is not even a problem if one of the original callers later needs to modify its sequence of calls, without the other callers needing the same modification. The caller with the new requirement can simply call A, B, and C, directly on the basis of its unique requirements. Yet D can still be called by the other original callers. Thus the addition of D does not seem to reduce the flexibility. On the other hand, the addition of D can often simplify likely changes, where all of the callers want the same change, namely, to how the lower modules are called. With D in the structure, that change can be made once instead of in each of the callers.

Eliminate "Funnel" Modules

Sometimes a module is designed which accomplishes no specific goal other than to pass data supplied by its caller to and from the modules it calls. The flow of data through the module looks something like an inverted funnel: the data from several modules below is collected and passed upwards through a single interface. Such modules are typically either logically or communicationally bound.

An example is the module PUT REPORTS X, Y, & Z in Figure 7.21. Here, the nonfunctionality is signaled by the "&" and the multiple objects in the module name. (An example where the nonfunctionality

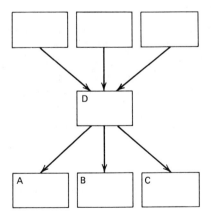

Figure 7.20 A possible simplification.

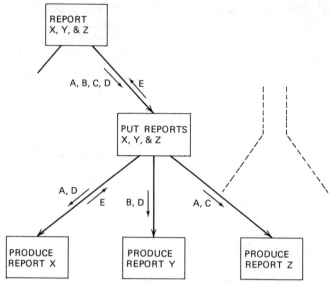

Figure 7.21   A funnel module.

might not be as obvious from the module name would be a module VALIDATE which calls VALIDATE A, VALIDATE B, and VALIDATE C.) PUT REPORTS X, Y, & Z accomplishes no real objective other than to gather the data of the modules it calls into one stream of data to be passed to its caller: REPORT X, Y, & Z. Note that the top module is also not functionally bound—though this is unavoidable because the specifications for the program were not functionally bound.

    There is a test that can detect—and eliminate—an inverted funnel. Determine one by one whether the modules the funnel module calls can be called directly from its caller. Check to see whether its caller already has the data necessary to call the lower modules, and make sure that the return data from the lower module is not needed within the funnel module. Whether the move will be justified depends on whether or not the coupling of the funnel module is reduced because of data parameters that no longer need to be passed to it. (In some cases it may be necessary to pass some of the remaining parameters *down to* the funnel module rather than *up from* it.) If each of the modules below can be successfully called from above, then eventually the funnel module will have no function except to pass data to a single module, at which point it can be eliminated.

In Figure 7.21, the module PRODUCE REPORT Z can be called directly from REPORT X, Y, & Z. The latter already contains the parameters A and C and there are no return parameters that PUT REPORTS X, Y, & Z needs. By calling PRODUCE REPORT Z from above, the parameter C can be eliminated from the interface to PUT REPORTS X, Y, & Z. This reduces the coupling of that interface while all other binding and coupling remains the same (except for the binding of PUT REPORTS X, Y, & Z, which has improved). Similarly, PRODUCE REPORT X can be called from REPORT X, Y, & Z. This further reduces the coupling to PUT REPORTS X, Y, & Z because the parameters A and E can be eliminated from the interface. Now all that PUT REPORTS X, Y, & Z does is to pass data to and from the module PRODUCE REPORT Y. PUT REPORTS X, Y, & Z can thus be eliminated: it is empty.

Modules that produce reports seldom return data to their caller. The parameter E being returned from PRODUCE REPORT X was included here for illustrative purposes because in other situations, funnel modules may call modules that return data to them.

The order in which modules can be eliminated is not necessarily arbitrary. In the example in Figure 7.21, attempts to eliminate the module PRODUCE REPORT X first would not have improved the coupling to the module PUT REPORTS X, Y, & Z. Although the functionality of module PUT REPORTS X, Y, & Z would have been improved, sometimes this is not as easy to detect (for example, when the name of the funnel module is VALIDATE). Thus, it is useful to examine *each* of the modules—or sometimes pairs of modules—called below to see if they can be called from above before deciding that this test for a funnel module has failed.

Funnel modules typically detect no return codes, issue no error messages, and do not recombine any of the data from the modules below them. They are an extra, unnecessary level within the structure that does not reduce the complexity. They actually *increase* the complexity because an unnecessary module must be coded, tested, and debugged.

When to Quit

How does the designer know when to stop looking for alternatives that may improve the structure? Look for the point of diminishing returns. Efforts to improve the structure should continue as long as the improvements save more effort than the designer spends making the improvements. The net effect will be to reduce the total cost of developing and implementing the program. While the effect of changes cannot be evaluated precisely, the designer can usually tell whether the improvements being made are substantial or whether they will have a rather minor effect.

One thing seems to happen toward the end of a design. Minor improvements seem to take the design in a "circle," resulting in the same chart as before the improvements. For example, consideration of one change to structure A makes structure B seem preferable (binding and coupling are the same). Another change makes structure C seem preferable to structure B. Then, when considering a third change, structure A seems preferable to structure C. The changes have taken the design around and back to the same structure again. This usually indicates that the structure is near the top of the improvement "hill" and that consideration of likely changes is simply taking the design around the top of the hill, while not making any substantial improvements.

The main idea is to identify when the point of diminishing returns has been reached. The objective of structured design is to reduce the cost of developing and maintaining programs. This objective is not reached by spending an excessive amount of time trying to achieve *the* ultimate and most functional structure. Thus, when a point of diminishing returns is reached, it is time to stop.

Checking Structure Charts

It is valuable to have structure charts checked by someone other than the designer. The following techniques are useful for checking other designers' charts and are also useful for checking your own charts.

Complete checking of a chart occurs on two different levels. One level is that the charts accurately satisfy the specifications. This requires a good understanding of the specifications and is usually best done by those already aware of the specifications and the requirements for the program. The other level of checking is whether additional improvements can be made to a chart based on structured design considerations. The latter checking can be done even without a detailed knowledge or understanding of the specifications by investigating three areas—parameters, functionality, and structure.

In order to check the *parameters* on an existing chart, check any module with more than five parameters. In fact, most modules should have three or fewer parameters, with ERROR and EOF parameters included in the count. Also, count every data element passed, whether passed as a separate parameter or not, except for arrays of related data and portions of externally defined records. Check also to see if any definitions for common data areas, such as control blocks, terminal work areas, or record definitions, are being copied into more than one module. Fields within terminal work areas and externally defined records should only be defined within one module (see section headed Passing Fields versus Records later in this chapter). Also, check any interfaces that include program switches. Ask why interfaces with program switches or too many parameters have to be that way. While there may occasionally be good reasons, most often program switches and too many parameters are signs that improvements are needed. In those few cases where there is a good reason, the reason is almost always a restriction on the part of the operating system or the programming language, or the need to interface to existing nonstructured code.

To check a structure chart for *functionality,* look at the name for each module. Check to see that the name implies a single function and that that function is implied by the structure of modules below the function. Question any module whose name does not clearly imply a single specific function or which has modules below it which do anything other than what is necessary to accomplish that specific function.

In order to check whether improvements could be made to the *structure* of an existing chart, check first to see if it has the form of the standard chart (see Chapter 7, "Standard Forms"). Also, check any modules that call more than three to five others, except for a transaction structure, and any modules *called by* more than three to five others, except for utility-type modules. Inquire as to whether any modules are expected to be significantly longer than about one page of executable code or if there are any modules that are not going to be separately compiled. Almost always, deficiencies in these areas of the structure indicate that improvements can be made.

SPECIAL CONSIDERATIONS

The topics in this section apply to specific situations rather than generally to all designs. Since these or similar situations could come up in any design, however, it is probably useful to read this section and to understand the topics and techniques explained here. The first two topics, for example, use a technique much more generally useful than just for the specific examples shown.

Program Parameters

Execution time parameters that are input to a program may seem to require many parameters to be passed throughout the structure. This is especially true if several different modules each need one or more of the input parameters. The tendancy may be to read the parameters in one module and then pass them as a group through the structure to the modules that finally need them. But this way all intervening modules end up with extra parameters in their interfaces because they are being used as a conduit to get the parameters to the final modules.

An alternative is shown in Figure 7.22. the PARM module reads the parameters from the input parameter cards. It returns individual

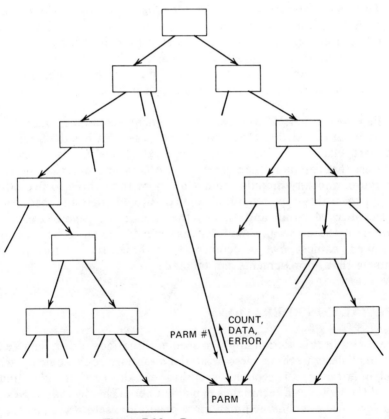

Figure 7.22   Program parameters.

parameters to specific modules, which call it requesting the parameter by number. A return set of parameters consisting of COUNT, DATA, and ERROR provides sufficient flexibility for passing most parameters. The COUNT can be used to return numeric items and the data parameter to return fixed data items. Variable numbers of items can be returned in the data parameter with the count indicating the number of items being returned. The PARM module can redefine the DATA parameter in order to place different kinds of numeric or alphabetic data within it. ERROR would, of course, indicate that the parameter requested was not available. Modules needing two or more parameters can call PARM twice.

Tables and Queues

The need to save and retrieve items from a table or a queue within a program can, like the previous case of program parameters, result in an apparent need to pass extra parameters throughout a structure. An example of such a situation is shown in Figure 7.23. ITEM and TABLE are input parameters for the module PUT IN TABLE. This is certainly a separate function from GET FROM TABLE. The parameters necessary for GET FROM TABLE are TABLE, KEY (for the item, if needed), and ITEM (returned to the caller). The difficulty is that TABLE must be passed through many module interfaces in order to be available for both of these calls. If TABLE is resident within one of the modules, the other one has to resort to an external connection (refer to "Types of Connections" in Chapter 6).

Before attempting to solve this kind of problem, first make sure that the problem exists. If the situation is such that the two table-handling modules are only called from the same module, then TABLE does not have to appear in any extra interfaces anyway.

If the problem does exist, one way to solve it is shown in Figure 7.24. Here, a TABLE module contains the table as well as code that will return the table address to a caller. If multiple tables are involved, an input parameter of table number would indicate which table was desired. This way, any caller can call either function without having to obtain the table address through its interface.

Not all languages allow addresses of parameters to be *returned* to their callers. One possible soluton to this restriction is shown in Figure 7.25, where PUT IN TABLE N, TABLE, and GET FROM TABLE N would all be written in assembler. The rest of the modules could still be written in the higher-level language.

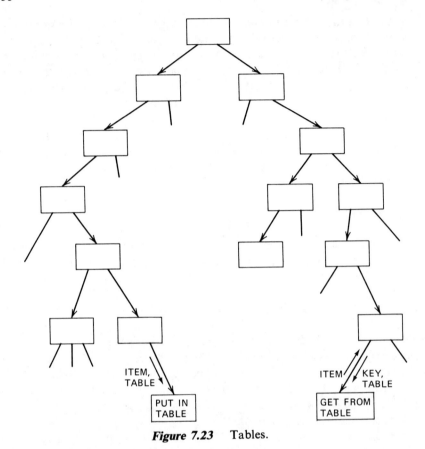

Figure 7.23   Tables.

Passing Fields versus Records

When a program reads a record and needs to pass the various fields throughout the structure, a question arises as to whether to pass the record as a single data item, or to pass the individual fields, each as a parameter. The answer varies, depending on the interface being considered within the structure. There is no single answer for all interfaces. Employing the widely used technique of passing the record and copying the record definition into every single module would result in having all modules common coupled. Any change to the record requires reconsideration of every module in the program. Further, errors in any module can cause the data in the record to be erroneously changed. Thus, all

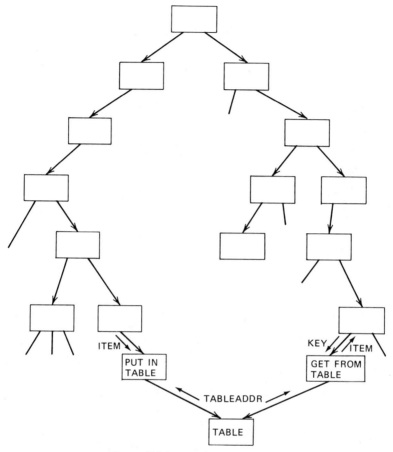

Figure 7.24 Reduced coupling.

modules in the program may have to be considered in order to fix such errors.

Choosing whether to pass a record or to pass fields involves making trade-offs among the following three benefits. First, the fewer the modules defining any given field from the record, the easier it is to adapt the structure to changes in the record. Ideally, any given field should be defined in only one module (it does not necessarily have to be the same module for all fields, though). Second, passing fewer fields in a record is simpler than passing extra (unnecessary) fields. The coupling is lower because less data is passed. Third, passing a record, or part of a

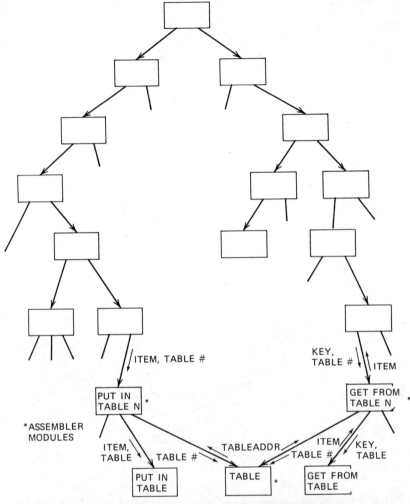

Figure 7.25   Solution for COBOL.

record, that is externally defined is simpler than passing each of the fields individually. The interface is less complicated because it is easier to use and understand.

Thus, the entire record should be passed to any module that does not use the fields in the records. The choice of passing the record or the fields to a module that *uses* the fields depends on the specific situation. If most of the fields in the record are needed, it will be simpler to pass the record. If very few are needed, then passing the fields results in passing less data. If, on the other hand, many fields are needed but they are side by side, then possibly a subrecord can be passed. Preferable subrecords are complete logical groupings of fields from the record, such as the renewal data, the name and address data, or the pricing data.

Another consideration is whether or not the caller has the field definition. If the caller already defines each of the fields in the record (for example, in order to pass them to other modules), then the fields should be passed; this reduces the number of modules that must define those particular fields. If one caller has the field definitions, but many fields must be passed through several levels which do not use the fields before reaching the module which needs the fields, then the tendency would again be to pass a record or sub-record.

This apparent need to trade off different advantages in order to arrive at the most preferable structure is unique. Binding and coupling complement one another. Improving the binding will improve the coupling (or at least not make it worse). Improving the coupling will improve the binding (or at least not make it worse). Making the structure of the solution match the structure of the real world typically improves both coupling and binding, and so on. But here, very uncharacteristically, it seems necessary to make trade-offs in order to arrive at the most preferable solution. This need to make trade-offs may be an indication that the whole technique of passing an entire record throughout a structure is not functionally sound. Instead, maybe the most preferable solution is to approach it in the same manner as was done above in program parameters and in tables. That is, to put the data in a module that is callable by whatever module wants it. This module would end up very much like the PARM module in the section above, "Program Parameters." It would contain the entire record and would pass individual fields to whatever modules requested them. In this manner, it would not be necessary to pass the entire record *or* a set of fields through many modules in the structure in order to reach the modules that needed the field(s). This is a somewhat dramatic deviation from how records are currently passed and, to the author's knowledge, has not been tried. Some data base products, though, do have the ability to support individual field access. This is an area where further investigation may be beneficial.

Buffers

Buffers can be used to decouple functions that are otherwise too highly coupled. Consider the reading of free-form input text, such as a compiler reading COBOL or PL/1 source code. Input records can have more than one phrase, and a phrase may span more than one input record. It may be difficult to see how to separate the functions of reading records from the function of obtaining phrases. One way to do this is to place a buffer between the two functions. The record-reading function puts records into the buffer. The phrase-obtaining function extracts phrases from the buffer. Buffers work in many cases when nothing else seems to be able to decouple highly coupled functions.

Isolate Nonfunctional Constraints

The environment may prevent a solution from being entirely functional. Examples are language restrictions, restrictions of the hardware or software system, because of the system design specifications, and/or because of the need to interface to existing code. If this happens, attempt to isolate this nonfunctionality to as few modules as possible.

COBOL, for example, requires that the READ, WRITE, OPEN, and CLOSE statements all be executed from the same compiled module. While this is no problem with respect to the READ and the OPEN or the WRITE and the CLOSE (since it is useful to have them in the same module anyway), having the READ and the WRITE in the same module will definitely result in a nonfunctional module. One suggestion is to produce a module with two entry points, one for READ and one for WRITE. Write the code for the two functions entirely separately, without overlapping any code. Do not share any local variables, except as absolutely necessary for the file definition. This way, it is possible to approximate closely the effect of having two entirely separate modules, even though they are compiled in the same module. This is not an example of control coupling as discussed in Chapter 6 in the section "What Is Communicated," where one module is contained within the *flow* of another module. In that case, executing the enclosing module executes the enclosed module. The suggestion here leaves the two control flows entirely separate.

An example of a hardware restriction might be a minicomputer that allows only 16 physical files with an application needing 17 logical files. On the basis of the file characteristics, the decision is made to have the seventeenth physically placed on the last half of file 13, which is expected to be small. A suggestion is to have only the I/O module know that the file 17 is actually placed on the last half of file 13. This way, the nonfunctional relationship between files 13 and 17 is isolated from the rest of the program. Then if the files are later rearranged—for example, file 17 is changed to share the last half of file 15 instead—only one module needs to be changed. This avoids the necessity of changing many places in the program that might otherwise have been coded to write to the last half of file 13.

Another example is a program which has to do more than one function. For example, it may have been decided that with one pass of a sequential file, two independent output reports are to be written by the same program. The top module of a program is always responsible for accomplishing the program's objectives. Thus, the functionality of the top module is limited to being not stronger than the functionality of the program specifications. In the example given here, the top module is communicationally bound at best. That is, its functions are to produce report 1 *and* report 2, which makes it a communicationally bound module because both are done from the same stream of data. Here, the suggestion is to limit the nonfunctionality to this one top module. This can be done by having one leg in the structure get the file and two distinct legs each producing one of the reports.

It may be necessary to interface to code that is nonfunctional. For example, there may be a requirement to use a generalized I/O module that is highly parameterized and/or includes control parameters. The module may need to be told when to open the file, what kind of processing to do, how to handle errors, etc.—all parameters that would usually be fixed for all calls within the same program. If this interface is used by many callers within the program, then each of the callers becomes highly connected to this nonfunctional module. One way to reduce this impact is to write an interface module. This interface module sets up all the unused or fixed parameters, leaving only the variable ones needed by the program. This way, only the one interface module is highly coupled to the original nonfunctional code, rather than all the callers having to pass extra, unnecessary parameters.

Reentrancy

Satisfying the need for modules to be reentrant may require adding parameters over and above those necessary in a batch (static) environment. *Any* new specification can result in a need for additional parameters, and reentrancy is another specification. It is unlikely that the simplest solution will automatically be reentrant. Thus, the designer should not spend undue time trying to find reentrant solutions to a program unless a reentrant solution is required. Some modules, such as EDIT NAME FIELD, may turn out to be reentrant (if the language compiler generates reentrant code). But a READ module that saves the open/closed status of the file in order to open it the first time (and be more like a black box), violates the reentrancy constraint against storing anything within itself.

One general solution to reentrancy requirements is to pass a reentrant work area from module to module. This constitutes only one additional parameter and can be used for storing reentrant modules' local variables. Do not, however, define the entire area in all modules or it will common-couple all the modules. Instead, allocate a different portion of the work area to each module. Each module can then allocate its portion of the work area without affecting other modules. Any module which uses up its portion is assigned an additional portion. In this way, changes to any given module do not affect other modules that also use the work area.

Larger Programs

One temptation is to feel that, although structured design is good for medium-sized programs, very large programs should not be broken down into modules as small as one page. The concern is that the complexity of having so many modules might outweigh the reduction in complexity achieved by dividing the program into modules.

This feeling is not only incorrect, but is even inconsistent with itself. Once very large programs have been (conceptually) broken into the large modules, these modules are each like a medium-sized program. But medium-sized programs benefit from being broken up into modules about one page in size.

Although writing many modules requires much effort, the effort to write very large programs is also large. But the code has to be written in either case. Structured design allows it to be written more independently, and thus with much less of the exponential growth in complexity that results as monolithic programs get larger.

SUMMARY

The overall approach of structured design is to build an initial chart that solves the specifications of the program. Then, identify items of binding and coupling that can be improved. In a step-by-step fashion, make changes to the structure that eliminate the identified items of binding and coupling. The initial structure is made primarily through attention to binding. Once the initial chart has been built, it is crucial to identify all of the parameters necessary to make the chart solve the specifications.

It is best if only one designer designs each structure chart. If there must be two designers, it is best if they *both* work on the complete structure chart. It is probably impractical to have three or more designers build a structure chart for one program. (A program is the code that executes as a result of an "execute" job control record or as a result of the depression of the ENTER key on an on-line system).

The majority of programs for business applications are variations of the basic structure shown in Figure 7.1. The chart in Figure 7.1 is the general structure for programs that get data from some place, do something with it, and then put it someplace—a typical business application. Since most programs end up having this structure, it is very helpful to assume this will be the case and to start with something in that form. Programs that do not fit this structure typically fit the structure shown in Figure 7.2. This is where a program does a variety of things depending on the type of transaction received. This can be the top structure of the program, or more commonly, it can occur at one of the levels in the structure in Figure 7.1.

One valuable technique for arriving at changeable structures is to match the structure of the program to the structure of the problem in the real world. The real world changes in accordance with its structure, independent of the structure chosen within the program. When the structure of the program matches the structure of the real world, then the chance that a simple change in the real world will cause a simple change within the program is enhanced.

When building an initial structure chart, err on the side of dividing too far. This facilitates identifying common functions. At the end of the structured design process, modules that still have only one caller, cannot be seen to be usable later, and do not simplify their caller can be merged into their caller.

The major guidelines for doing structured design are independence, simplicity, and observability. Independence allows the parts of the program to be debugged, understood, fixed, and changed relatively independent of the rest of the program. Simplicity is achieved primarily through the independence of the modules. Simplicity is not synonymous with "fewest lines of code" (this can probably only be achieved by extreme optimization). Instead, it means that the complexity is reduced—and this is done by breaking down the large complex problem into smaller simple ones.

Observability measures how easy it is to see why the program does what it does. In most cases, observability is improved by simply picking the alternative that is clear—like picking descriptive names for parameters rather than nondescriptive ones—and usually it is something that does not have to be traded off with performance.

Although the name of a module should explicitly include the function to be performed, there are elements that do not need to be included explicitly in the name. These include returning ERROR and EOF parameters. Also, if the specifications require reporting detailed actions that take place within a module, then the CALL to a WRITE TO LOG or WRITE TO AUDIT FILE module should also be made from within the module where the detail actions take place. Other implicit elements of a module include performing error recovery and issuing error messages relevant to that module's function.

Anything that enhances the ability to use a module without having to inspect the code within it first improves the usability, flexibility, and understandability of the program. A clear name for the module and its parameters, a good prologue, and a logical order for the parameters can all enhance the program's "black-box" characteristic—the ability to be used without its insides being viewed.

A major goal of structured design is to avoid duplicating functions. Implementing the same function, such as "edit name field," more than once in a program wastes development *and* maintenance time. Not only must each of the occurrences be programmed and debugged, but maintenance to any of the occurrences must be coordinated with maintenance to all other occurrences if they are to be kept in synchronization. Often, though, the maintenance programmer is not even *aware* of all the occurrences of the same function.

It is surprising how often duplicate functions are put into programs. They result from things like including code to edit the name field that is the third one in the master record, and then later including new code to edit the name field that is the first field on the transaction record. A separately compiled module can edit either name field when they are passed as a parameter. One technique for eliminating duplicate functions in modules which seem similar but are not exactly alike is to extract the part that is common to both of them. Then check to see if what is left in either of the original two modules should be merged back into their callers.

Implementing each specification in only one module is similar to eliminating duplicate functions. Implementing each specification in only one module reduces the chance that changes to the specification will require changes to more than one module. One of the primary advantages of low coupling (and high binding) is the resulting change-ability of the program. This changeability enhances testing and maintenance by making it easier to make changes, both to fix an error and to implement a new requirement. When the binding and coupling of two alternatives are the same, changeability may serve as a criteria for choosing between them. Changeability is also a useful criterion for testing final designs. Test changeability by evaluating the impact of changes that are likely to occur. Any difficulties that would arise in adapting to reasonable changes will probably highlight binding and coupling problems not previously identified.

Solutions can often be made dramatically simpler just by concentrating on finding the simplest alternative. It is unfortunate how much unnecessary complexity results from designing based on premature attention to performance considerations or to presumed future needs. It is easier to achieve the best performance by designing the simplest solution first. Then, if that does not already run fast enough, look for ways to trade off the minimum complexity for the maximum performance. This usually results in solutions that are *both* simpler and faster—and it takes less time to do both. Often, there is a temptation to provide for flexibility requirements by trying to generalize functions beyond what is needed today or by trying to add future functions today. But all future requirements cannot possibly be implemented now. And many turn out to be different when they finally occur. Adding those functions today complicates the current solution. This makes it harder to make changes and thus *reduces* flexibility, instead of increasing it. Moreover, since the future requirements are almost always ill defined, they are the hardest to provide for and result in more time spent and more complexity introduced than the specifications that have been approved and defined. Flexibility is achieved not through trying to provide for the function now, but instead by choosing alternatives that *allow* the function to be added later. Flexibility is also enhanced by *not* implementing unnecessary requirements, as this complicates the current solution, making it less changeable and thus less flexible.

Once a function is written, it should be available for wherever it is needed. Thus, calls across levels are not only acceptable but desirable. There is no "level of importance" attached to any level within the structure that dictates on what level any module must reside or restricts calls from going more than one level. Just watch for recursion when calling *up* across levels if the programming language does not allow for recursion.

Modules often need to be able to signal to their callers that they cannot perform their function. This can usually be done through a binary status parameter such as ERROR, which is returned to the caller. Only the immediate caller, however, should need to know that the called module encountered an error. The caller may set *its* error parameter on as a result, but it should not pass along errors from lower-level modules also.

ERROR and EOF are parameters many modules need to pass to their callers. It is counterproductive to spend much time trying to eliminate them. Nonetheless, when ERROR or EOF parameters can be eliminated, is does reduce the coupling.

Initialization parameters can usually be eliminated. If the need to initialize one or more modules in the structure is unavoidable, then at least do all initialization calls from only one module, which is called from the top module. This is preferable to making all modules in the structure interrelated by having them initialize each other. It is also probably simpler to have a second entry point into a module for initialization. This way the main entry point is not complicated for all other callers by an initialization parameter.

READ modules are valuable. They can isolate program(s) from changes in a file. The data in a record can be extended, rearranged, or even split across multiple files. By changing the READ module to reconstruct the old format, it is easy to make all programs work with a new file. It is also convenient to have a WRITE ERROR module. This is a single place where any desired changes in how error messages are to be written can be implemented. A PRINT module is a convenient place to implement spooling capabilities for systems that do not provide them. All three modules should open and close their own files. Thus they are useful even if merely because they make rewriting this logic for each new program unnecessary.

Program switches are a way for one module to tell another module what to do. Note that program switches are not always binary, nor are binary parameters always program switches. There is always an alternative (unless specifically excluded by the environment) that eliminates the need for a program switch. Thus, a program switch is at best an extra, unnecessary parameter. But the worst problem of having a program switch is that it increases the likelihood that errors made in one module can cause another module to fail. Switches passed downwards indicate that the receiving module can do more than one function—otherwise, why pass the switch? A solution is to put each function in a separate module.

Switches passed upward indicate that there is code somewhere in the structure above the module setting the switch that is conditionally executed based on the switch. One approach for eliminating these switches is to identify the dependent code and move it downwards in the structure, move the decision upwards in the structure, or do both.

Three requirements must be satisfied in order to justify leaving one module pulled out of another at the end of the design.

1 It must be functional.

2 It must be low-coupled.

3 a) It is usable from two places (now or later), and/or
b) It simplifies an overly complex caller.

The issue in reducing coupling is to reduce the number or complexity of parameters passed to a given module. The creation of a new interface, which occurs when a module is extracted from its caller, is not a coupling issue. Similarly, adding another caller for a module does not increase the coupling (even though there is a new call and new parameters are written on the chart). From a coupling point of view, each module has only one interface. The issue is whether or not the coupling for that one interface can be reduced.

Functions are always made up of elements. Elements or subfunctions could potentially be extracted as yet new modules. The decomposition process can stop when a size is achieved that can be handled fairly easily. This is approximately one listing page or less of executable code (or only 15 to 30 lines if APL). There are examples of larger (functionally bound) modules which cannot be broken into pieces without increasing the complexity. Typically, these either have no conditional branches in them or have very simple logic, for example, a single structured programming CASE structure. Any modules larger than about one page of code should be examined, though, to see if they are too complex, and to see whether or not a functional module can be extracted that will reduce the complexity.

Modules with less than one to five lines of executable code should be examined to see if they justifiably reduce the complexity of the caller. Functional modules that are low coupled and called from more than one place (either now or potentially in the future) should always be kept, regardless of their size. Such a module can serve as a single place to make a single change that can take effect for the entire program. There should be no great concern over the fact that such modules are small. Indeed, the optimal situation would be if all functions could be implemented in just a few lines of code—that would make everything easy.

It is unusual to have a module call more than three to five others, although there are examples where it is all right, such as the transaction structure (Figure 7.2). Conversely, for other than utility modules, it is unusual to have a module *called by* more than three to five others. It is a good idea to check any occurrence of a module either calling or being called by more than three to five others, to see if it results from problems within the structure. In both types of cases, check especially for binding problems within the module in question. Typically, the module will be trying to do more than one thing and can be broken apart either sideways or vertically into two or more modules.

Sometimes during the development of a structure it is noted that a set of modules is called in the same sequence from multiple places. It may be useful to create a new module simply to contain that calling sequence, if any kind of functional name can be found for such a module. The module can serve as a single place to change the calling sequence for all callers.

Sometimes a module is designed that has no function itself but simply passes data from the caller above to the called programs below. It acts somewhat like an "inverted funnel." See if each of the modules called below the funnel module can be called directly from the funnel module's caller. If this can be done successfully for each of the called modules, the funnel module can be eliminated.

It is time to quit structured design when it takes more time to make a change to the design than will be saved by the change—i.e., at the point of diminishing returns. Another sign that the design is near the end is if successive small changes take the design around in a "circle" back to a previous structure.

Passing run-time parameters to the appropriate modules in a program may seem to require passing the parameters through many interfaces. An alternative is to have a PARM module that reads the input parameters. Any module needing a parameter calls PARM, specifying the number for the parameter it wants.

A similar situation arises when a program needs to put data in a table and to get data from it. Since PUT and GET are different functions, they should be different modules. It may seem that the only way to then give the two modules access to the same table is to pass the table address throughout the entire structure. An alternative is shown in Figure 7.24. Here, a TABLE module contains the table and will return its address to any caller.

When dealing with records within a program, a question arises as to whether to pass the record as a single parameter or to pass the fields within it, each as individual parameters. Three different objectives must be balanced. The first is that passing an externally defined record as a single parameter is simpler than passing each of the fields as individual parameters. Second, passing fewer fields reduces the coupling. The third objective is to have as few modules as possible in a program contain the description of any one set of fields within the record.

As a result, the advantage tends to be on the side of passing the record when most or all of the fields need to be passed anyway, when the needed fields are grouped together within the record (in which case a subrecord can be passed), or when the fields would be passed through a module that does not need them. The advantage tends to be on the side of passing the individual fields when only a few fields are needed, when the needed fields are not side by side within the record, or when the module passing the fields needs to have the field definition in it for other reasons anyway.

This unique circumstance of having to trade off different objectives may indicate that passing records among modules in a structure is inappropriate to begin with. A simpler solution may be to have a module that can return requested fields to any caller. That module reads the record and is then the only one that contains the record and its field definitions.

Buffers can be useful to decouple functions that otherwise seem to be too highly coupled. Whenever it is difficult to see how to separate functions, consider whether or not buffering can be used to solve the problem.

Sometimes external constraints require a program to be nonfunctional. Examples are nonfunctional specifications and existing control-coupled interfaces. Attempt to isolate as much code as possible from any nonfunctionality. See if an interface module can isolate the rest of the program from the nonfunctionality.

Re-entrancy is an extra restriction on the implementation of a program (i.e., the simplest modules are often not automatically re-entrant). Thus, re-entrancy requirements may cause extra complexity, often in the form of an added parameter. In an on-line system, for example, a terminal work area is usually required. Modules can usually be made reentrant by passing them the terminal work area so they can define their local variables within it.

Structured design is just as appropriate for very large programs as for medium-sized ones—even though more modules result as the module size is kept at about one page. It would be inconsistent if very large programs should only be broken into very large modules. This is because according to structured design principles, the very large modules—programs—are themselves simpler when done as about one-page modules.

8

An Example of Improving a Structure Chart

The use of structured design concepts in evaluating alternatives to improve a structure chart will be illustrated by taking a sample structure chart through to the final design. The program is a patient-monitoring program. (See Stevens et al., 1974. In that article, the derivation of the design was not described.) The specifications for the program are described below.

A patient-monitoring program is required for a hospital. Patients in the wing for the critically ill can be monitored by a device that measures factors such as pulse, temperature, blood pressure, and skin resistance. The program reads these factors on a periodic basis and stores them in a data base that is accessed by patient number. Safe ranges for each factor are specified by each patient's doctor (e.g., patient X's safe temperature range is 97 to 104 degrees Fahrenheit). If a factor falls outside of a patient's safe range, or if an analog device fails, the nurses' station is to be notified. Messages regarding factors outside a patient's safe range should specify the patient number. Messages regarding measurement device failures are to indicate the bed number. Analogue devices are read by the hardware on the basis of bed number.

The factors are read as a stream of seven measurements followed by an error-flag word. The first seven bits in the error-flag word indicate, for each of the factors respectively, whether the hardware has detected any device failures such as a measuring unit being unplugged. The program should also check whether or not measurements lie within a reasonable range—even though the hardware has indicated they are valid. Any invalid measurements stored in the data base should be flagged to indicate that they were detected to be invalid. However, the safe/unsafe interpretations for the factors are not to be stored in the data base. The factors themselves are totally independent of one another and, in fact, differ in format and length (i.e., they are a mixture of floating-point and fixed-point measurements of varying lengths).

An Initial Chart

An initial structure is shown in Figure 8.1. It is intended to be what someone *not* skilled in structured design might produce, so there will be ample room to show how initial charts can be improved. Referring to the module OBTAIN FACTORS in Figure 8.1, a patient number (PN) is used to identify each set of factors. EOF signals when the last patient has been read for this pass. ERROR FLAGS indicate failure(s) of measurement device(s).

Modules are called from CHECK FACTORS to do three functions:

1   Detect invalid measurements (ERROR FLAGS 2—out of reasonable range).
2   Identify safe ranges for a given patient.
3   Determine if any factors for this patient are unsafe.

DETECT UNSAFE FACTORS sets UNSAFE FLAGS off if ERROR FLAGS (0 Red with ERROR FLAGS 2 in CHECK FACTORS) indicates a particular factor to be erroneous.

HANDLE FACTORS causes the factors to be stored in the data base and the nurse's station to be notified of unsafe factors and/or measurement device failures.

There is one specification not met by this initial chart. Messages about measurement device failures should indicate the bed number. But NOTIFY STN OF BAD DEVICE (notify station of bad device) is being passed the patient number. This specification will have to be met later in order for the final structure to solve all the specifications.

Improving the Solution

Improvements can be made to this structure using binding and coupling concepts and the suggestions from Chapter 7. Improvements can gener-

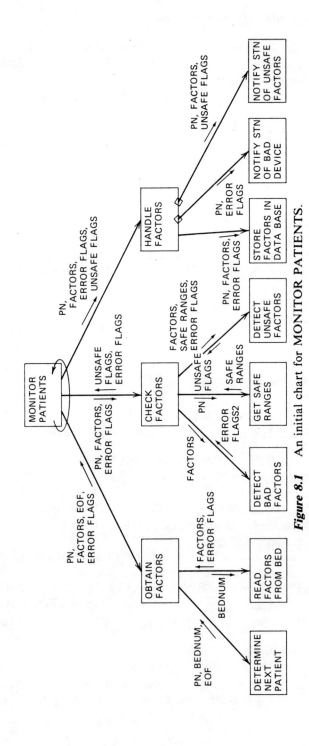

Figure 8.1 An initial chart for MONITOR PATIENTS.

ally be made in any order. The order chosen here may be different from the order in which the reader perceives possible improvements.

First, the interface between MONITOR PATIENTS and HANDLE FACTORS can be simplified. UNSAFE FLAGS are not used within HANDLE FACTORS except to be passed to NOTIFY STN OF UNSAFE FACTORS. The latter returns no parameters needed by HANDLE FACTORS, and MONITOR PATIENTS has all the parameters needed to call NOTIFY STN OF UNSAFE FACTORS directly. By so doing, the parameter UNSAFE FLAGS can be eliminated in the interface to HANDLE FACTORS. See Figure 8.2.

By the same logic, MONITOR PATIENTS has all of the parameters necessary to call STORE FACTORS IN DATA BASE directly. By so doing, the parameter FACTORS can be eliminated in the call to HANDLE FACTORS. This again reduces the coupling on one interface within the structure. See Figure 8.3.

HANDLE FACTORS now has no function other than simply to call NOTIFY STN OF BAD DEVICE. Thus, it can now be eliminated. See Figure 8.4.

Closer inspection of HANDLE FACTORS in Figure 8.1 will indicate that it had very little function to start with. In particular, it was communicationally bound at best and was simply a "funnel" module, as

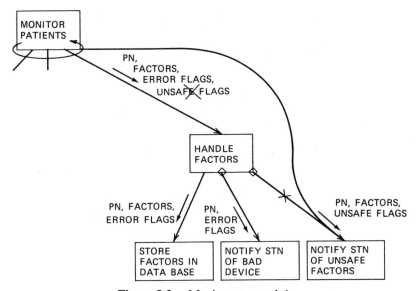

Figure 8.2 Moving one module.

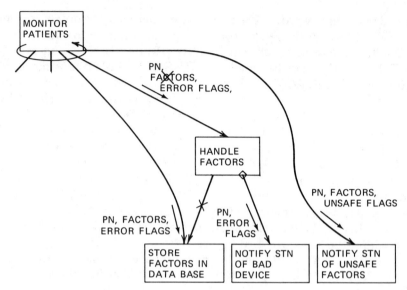

Figure 8.3   Moving a second module.

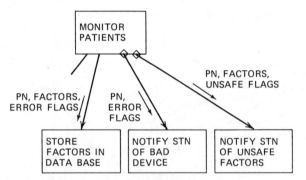

Figure 8.4   Funnel module eliminated.

discussed in Chapter 7 in "Eliminate 'Funnel' Modules." Its only use was as a conduit for data from its caller to the modules it called. No function was actually accomplished within HANDLE FACTORS—as evidenced by the fact that each module beneath it could be called by MONITOR PATIENTS without eliminating any parameters needed within HANDLE FACTORS itself.

Since NOTIFY STN OF BAD DEVICE must issue a message that

contains bed number rather than patient number a way to satisfy the requirement is for it to translate patient number to bed number. This may be done, for example, by accessing the data based by patient number and retrieving the bed number. This is the same as a function performed with DETERMINE NEXT PATIENT. One way to elimate this duplicate function is to pass bed number up to MONITOR PATIENTS and then down to NOTIFY STN OF BAD DEVICE. This increases the coupling of OBTAIN FACTORS, but is justified because it eliminates duplicate functions, as was discussed in Chapter 7 in "Avoid Duplicating Functions." The parameter is also an explicit item which may be easier to get rid of than trying to eliminate the duplicate function in one step (Figure 8.5).

BEDNUM can now be eliminated from the call to OBTAIN FACTORS by calling NOTIFY STN OF BAD DEVICE directly from READ FACTORS FROM BED. This reduces the coupling by eliminating a parameter (see "Size of Connections" in Chapter 6). In order to do this properly, however, it will be necessary to call DETECT BAD FACTORS from READ FACTORS FROM BED also so that the station will still be notified of factors found to be bad either by the hardware or by the software. See Figure 8.6. This also simplifies the interface to CHECK FACTORS by eliminating the need to return updated ERROR FLAGS. While it does not eliminate a *parameter* from the call statement, it does reduce the complexity of the interface and, thus, the coupling. The chart is now as shown in Figure 8.7. Notice that this move might never have been noticed if different designers were all developing different legs of this same structure chart independently. This is why it is important always to work with the complete chart.

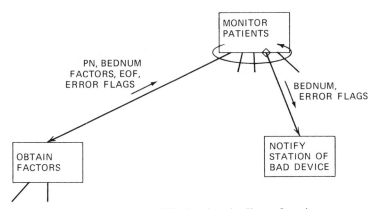

Figure 8.5   Eliminating duplicate function.

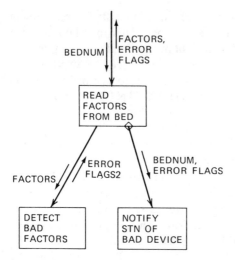

Figure 8.6   Coupling reduced.

NOTIFY STN OF BAD DEVICE and NOTIFY STN OF UNSAFE FACTORS both must write lines to the station. Since no module is available (with this particular computer) to write a line to a station, the preceding modules will have duplicate function within them. Further, the characteristics of the station, or even the device itself, may change in the future. Thus, for the purposes of both eliminating duplicate function and enhancing the ability to accommodate likely changes, a module is added that can write a line to the station. See Figure 8.8. (In Chapter 7, see "Avoid Duplicating Functions" and "Opt for Changeability.")

Depending on the complexity involved in the module NOTIFY STN OF UNSAFE FACTORS, a module to format an unsafe line can be pulled out, as shown in Figure 8.9. This module is justified strictly by the size and complexity expected of NOTIFY STN OF UNSAFE FACTORS, since FORMAT UNSAFE LINE is not likely to be usable from any other place now or later (see "Extracting a Module From Its Caller" in Chapter 7).

BEDNUM can be eliminated from the interface to DETERMINE NEXT PATIENT if the module READ FACTORS FROM BED does the translation of patient number to bed number itself. This reduces the coupling. Given the complexity of READ FACTORS FROM BED, this is best done in a separate module, as shown in Figure 8.10. BEDNUM is replaced by PN (patient number) in the interface to READ FACTORS FROM BED (this does not change the coupling

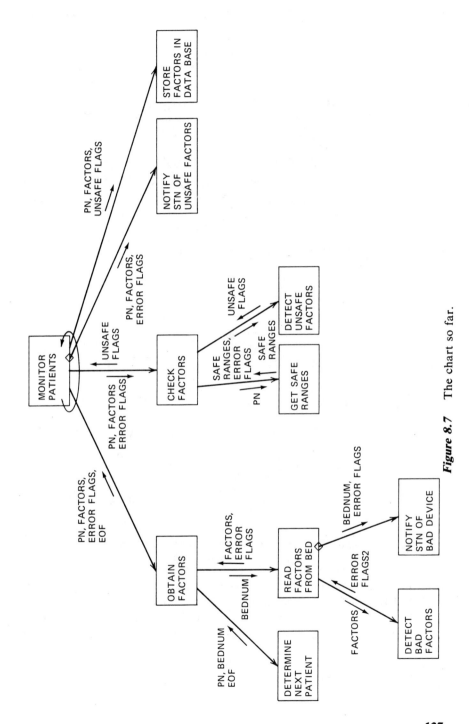

Figure 8.7 The chart so far.

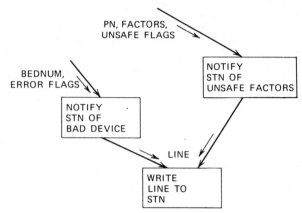

Figure 8.8   Duplicate function eliminated.

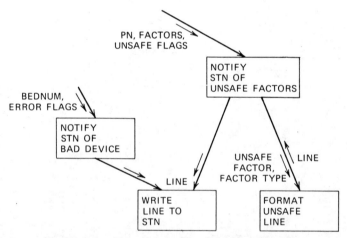

Figure 8.9   Extracting a module from its caller.

there). Note that the new interface to the new module PATIENT
NUMBER TO BEDNUM is not an issue when evaluating coupling.
This interface is justified by the concepts of extracting a module from
its caller. (See "Extracting a Module From Its Caller" in Chapter 7.)
And, regardless of whether a separate module was identified, the movement of the patient number to bed number translation from the
module DETERMINE NEXT PATIENT to the module READ FAC-

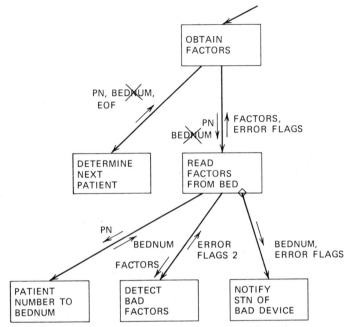

Figure 8.10   Reduced coupling to DETERMINE NEXT PATIENT.

TORS FROM BED is justified because it reduces coupling to DETER-
MINE NEXT PATIENT. READ FACTORS FROM BED, however,
is no longer a proper description of that module since patient number
rather than bed number is now passed to it. A better name might be
OBTAIN PATIENT FACTORS.

The code that reads factors given a bed number is now hidden within
OBTAIN PATIENT FACTORS. It may be useful in the future to have
that code—which must be written anyway— available at an interface.
For example, the repair persons who fix the measuring devices may wish
to interface to code that can read from a bed. Since there may not even
be a patient in the bed when they want to try the read, the read would
have to be done on the basis of bed number. This interface can be made
available (again) by pulling a module READ FACTORS FROM BED
down out of OBTAIN PATIENT'S FACTORS, as shown in Figure
8.11 This is justified as per the section "Opt for Changeability" in
Chapter 7.

The module PATIENT NUMBER TO BED NUMBER could have
been created to eliminate the duplicate function in DETERMINE

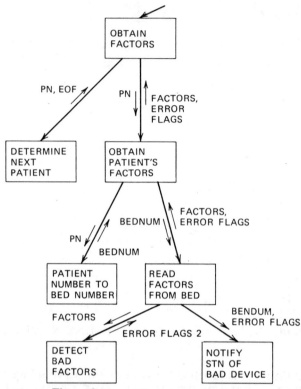

Figure 8.11   Allowing for flexibility.

NEXT PATIENT and NOTIFY STATION OF BAD DEVICE earlier (if the alternative was seen at that point). Notice that the module eventually resulted anyway.

Based on the size and complexity of READ FACTORS FROM BED, it no longer seems necessary for DETECT BAD FACTORS to be a separate module. Thus, it can be merged into READ FACTORS FROM BED. (See "Extracting a Module From Its Caller" in Chapter 7.)

The structure chart now is as in 8.12. This is basically the same structure (though with somewhat different names for the modules) as that shown in the original article, *Structured Design* (Stevens et al., 1974), except for the position of STORE FACTORS IN DATA BASE. In that solution, the latter was called from OBTAIN FACTORS.

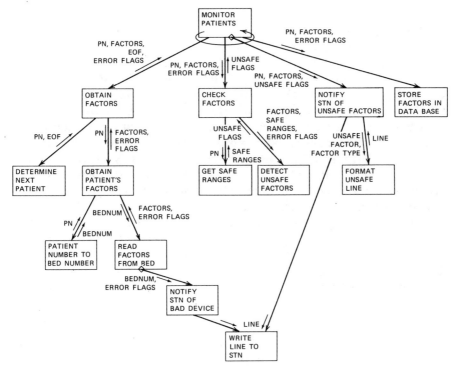

Figure 8.12   An intermediate solution.

However, that made OBTAIN FACTORS not functionally bound since it really was OBTAIN FACTORS AND STORE THEM IN THE DATA BASE. The position of STORE FACTORS IN DATA BASE in Figure 8.12 is an improvement since it eliminates the binding problem of OBTAIN FACTORS in the earlier solution.

Further Improvements

NOTIFY STN OF BAD DEVICE issues an error message on the basis of error flags returned from READ FACTORS FROM BED to its caller. Typically (as discussed in "Elements of a Functional Module," in Chapter 7), it is more flexible to issue such error messages from the caller. In fact, considering the need to test devices that have been fixed, it is probably desirable to avoid having the station notified every time the analog unit is tested and still found to be failing. Thus, the structure seems more usable if NOTIFY STN OF BAD DEVICE is called from OBTAIN PATIENT'S FACTORS rather than from READ FACTORS FROM BED (Figure 8.13).

The parameter UNSAFE FLAGS returned from CHECK FACTORS can be eliminated if CHECK FACTORS calls NOTIFY STN OF UNSAFE FACTORS directly (Figure 8.14). As is typical when moving a module, the interface to NOTIFY STN OF UNSAFE FACTORS is unchanged. However, justified moves often reduce the coupling of either the moved module's original caller or its new caller. Now the name CHECK FACTORS no longer adequately describes that module's function. REPORT UNSAFE FACTORS is a more descriptive name for what occurs between when it is called and when it returns. The chart is now as in Figure 8.15.

The next change can be justified strictly on the basis of reduced coupling. It can also be seen to reduce the complexity within the structure, as well as to improve the adaptability of this program to future possible changes.

Many of the interfaces contain the parameters FACTORS and/or

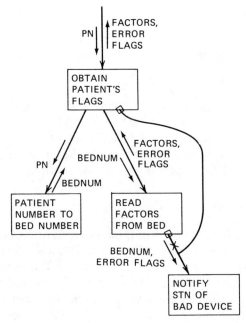

Figure 8.13   Designing for future changes.

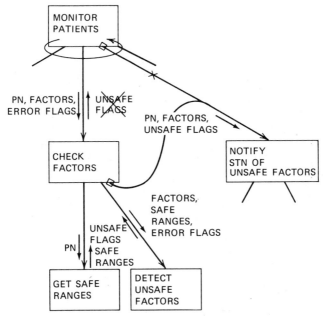

Figure 8.14 Reducing coupling to CHECK FACTORS.

ERROR FLAGS. Each of these parameters represents seven somewhat similar, but basically unrelated, data items. Note, for example, that the error flags are more related to the factors they represent than they are to each other. The factors themselves are of different lengths and data types. Interfaces containing both FACTORS and ERROR FLAGS thereby contain fourteen data items. This number can be reduced by passing one factor at a time, along with a factor-type indicator and one error parameter. Such an interface would contain three data items instead of the fourteen.

Most important, this change reduces the number of modules dependent on the number, types, and arrangements of factors sent back by the measuring devices at each bed. READ FACTORS FROM BED, DETECT UNSAFE FACTORS, REPORT UNSAFE FACTORS and NOTIFY STN OF UNSAFE FACTORS all contain code dependent upon the arrangement, types, and number of factors. It also seems likely that new measuring units may be added later. These new measuring units may measure the same factors in a different order, different factors, additional factors, or some combination of the preceding. Each

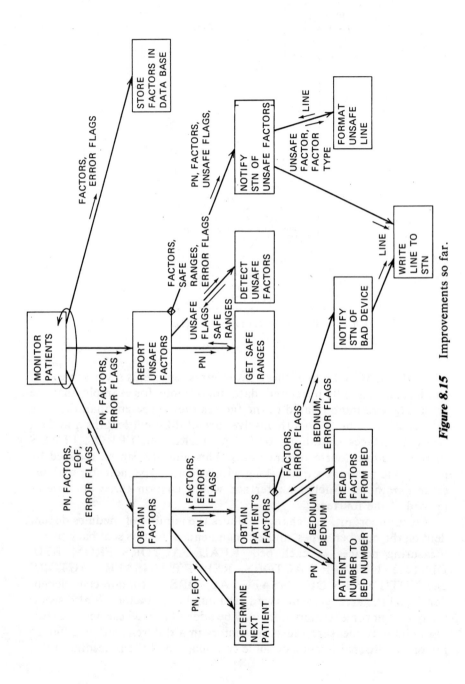

Figure 8.15 Improvements so far.

factor arrangement will further complicate each of the modules identified as being dependent upon the factor types and arrangement.

This situation is very similar to the one described in Chapter 7, "Implement Each Specification in Only One Module." The code that is dependent on the number and arrangement of factors can be isolated to the single module READ FACTORS FROM BED by having that module deblock the factors and send them back one at a time with a factor-type indicator. The loops for handling each of the factors in the modules DETECT UNSAFE FACTORS, REPORT UNSAFE FACTORS, and NOTIFY STN OF UNSAFE FACTORS can be eliminated. The names of the modules in the structure are now changed to indicate that they deal with a single factor rather than factors. It is also necessary for READ FACTOR FROM BED to return a factor-end-of-file (FEOF) once the last factor has been returned for that bed. Similarly, OBTAIN PATIENT'S FACTOR returns FEOF to its caller. In both cases, a single factor is returned as long as patient number and bed number respectively are the same on input. Upon detecting FEOF, the caller knows it is time to send a new key. The caller can send a new key earlier if it decides to do so, or it can request the same bed again. The result is shown in Figure 8.16, which includes one other change, which will be discussed next.

DETECT UNSAFE FACTOR now only identifies whether a single number is within a specified range. It and REPORT UNSAFE FACTOR are so simple that DETECT UNSAFE FACTOR can no longer be justified on the basis of simplifying REPORT UNSAFE FACTORS. Thus, it has been merged into its caller.

It could be argued on the same basis that FORMAT UNSAFE LINE could now be merged into NOTIFY STN OF UNSAFE FACTORS. Whether or not this should be done depends on the complexity—and thus possibly the programming language—of the module NOTIFY STN OF UNSAFE FACTOR.

Each different factor stream coming from new measuring instruments will complicate the module READ FACTOR FROM BED. In any solution, however, there must be code that is able to recognize and interpret different factor streams. In this solution, only one module is dependent on, and affected by, changes in those specifications.

It may further simplify the structure to have READ FACTOR FROM BED translate each factor into the same data format and length. Doing this depends upon whether it is acceptable to store and analyze the data in its original form or in a form that may contain data conversion inaccuracy.

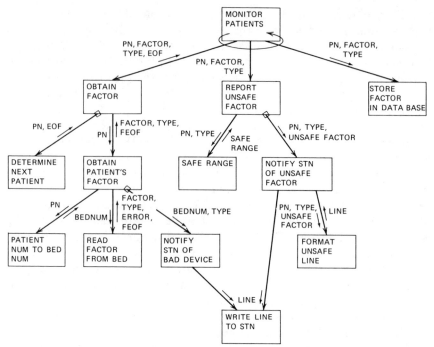

Figure 8.16   The last chart.

It may be noted that the performance of STORE FACTOR IN DATA BASE has been degraded substantially, since it writes seven times as many records: one per factor. This performance can be regained, however—and with minimal additional complexity—by buffering the factors for each patient number until a new patient number is received. An end-of-file will have to be passed to STORE FACTOR IN DATA BASE to store the factors for the last patient. If these I/O's can be overlapped with the rest of the processing anyway, even adding this minimal amount of complexity may not be justified. In any case, this approach—giving up a small amount of complexity to get the performance back—is greatly preferable to being reluctant to change FACTORS and ERROR FLAGS into FACTOR, TYPE, and ERROR. That reluctance would result in losing the benefits of adaptability to new factor types and quantities. But it would not achieve any better performance than that achieved through the relatively trivial change to buffer factors within the module STORE FACTOR IN DATA BASE.

The problem with the original structure in Figure 8.1 may now be more readily identified. The original structure tried to get all data on the left, do all processing in the middle, and produce all output on the right. This kind of structure tends to suffer from logical or communicational binding. Software detection of incorrect factors and notifying the station of incorrect factors are both more closely associated with the hardware detection of incorrect factors than they are with checking factors and storing factors respectively. (The initial structure for this example was developed that way intentionally. This provided a fertile ground for improvement so that the technique of improving existing structure charts could be better demonstrated.)

Similar problems apply to structures that group initialize, process, and terminate functions. In fact, such cases have even stronger functional relationships between the initialize and terminate modules, and the functions they initialize and terminate. Thus, even stronger reasons would exist for rearranging the structure to get those highly related elements together than are present in the previous case.

Summary

This chapter illustrates how to improve an initial structure chart. The example used is the patient monitoring program from *Structured Design* (Stevens et al., 1974). The tips and techniques used during the process of improving the initial structure include:

- Eliminating a "funnel" module
- Eliminating duplicate functions
- Reducing coupling
- Extracting a module from its caller
- Compressing a module into its caller
- Designing for future changes
- Issuing an error message from the caller of the module that detects it

The movement of modules from one side of the structure to another in the course of this process illustrates why it is valuable to work with a complete structure chart, rather than having several designers work on the structure chart independently.

The technique used most frequently was to reduce coupling by making a change in the structure which eliminated a parameter from at least one interface in the structure.

9

Generating an Initial Chart

Any structure chart that implements the specifications of the program can serve as an initial chart. Improvements can be made to it in a step-by-step fashion to reach the final structure, independent of the quality of the initial structure. On the other hand, the better the quality of the initial structure, the less work will have to be done in order to do the rest of the design. The basic process suggested here is to start with a top module and then add single-function modules below it as needed to satisfy the specifications. Binding is the most useful measure during this process, but coupling can be considered whenever it helps the designer choose between alternatives.

An approach that can save considerable design time is to assume that the structure of the program will match one of the variations of the common structure for input/process/output types of programs as discussed in "Standard Forms" in Chapter 7 (see Figure 9.1). Most business programs fit this structure or one of its variations. Thus, it will be easier if this structure is assumed to be correct. Then, for those few programs where another type of structure is preferable, this structure can be improved and transformed into that one. But if unique structures are built for each program, much time may be wasted improving these structures into the common form.

In building the common structure, the first thing to identify is the "top." That is not to say the top *module*, since that can be defined for any program immediately. The top module's function is DO IT. The top

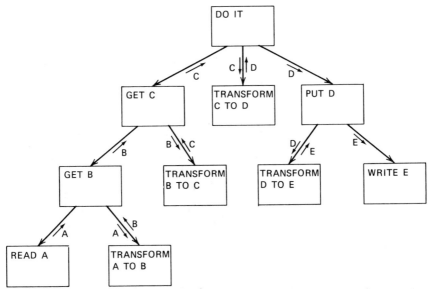

Figure 9.1 Common structure for input/process/output types of programs.

module is responsible for making sure that the program specifications are accomplished. The question is, what are the functions of the modules called from the top module? What follows is a heuristic way of identifying the "top." The steps are basically the following:

1 Draw a data-flow diagram for the program.
2 Eliminate all streams of data that are not major ones.
3 Find the "middle" of the data-flow diagram.
4 Based on that, create the two top levels.
5 Expand the rest of the chart, on the basis primarily of binding concepts.

Draw a Data-Flow Diagram

The first step is to draw a data-flow diagram for the major external stream(s) of data. A data-flow diagram is a chart indicating the flows of data and the processes that act on that data. Data-flow diagrams are not new. Systems flowcharts, which are drawn to show how systems of programs interrelate, are data-flow diagrams (see Figure 9.2). Currently, most data-flow diagrams exclude the symbols that indicate the form

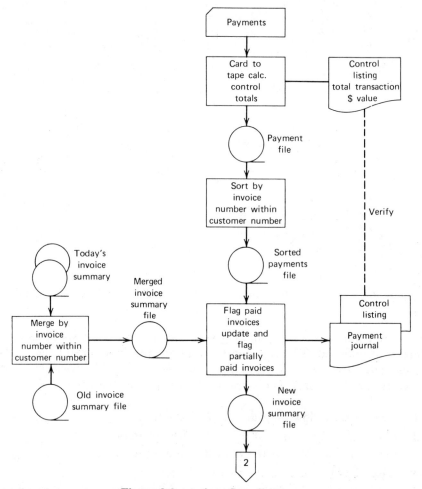

Figure 9.2   A data-flow diagram.

of the data (e.g., tape, card, disk, or printing) and simply indicate beside the arrow what data flows from process to process. Circles are often used to denote processes.

Figure 9.3 shows a data-flow diagram for a program whose objective is to calculate the optimal mix of meat within a hotdog. This example came from Larry Constantine and is an excellent one for showing how to build an initial structure. The idea is to find the least-cost combina-

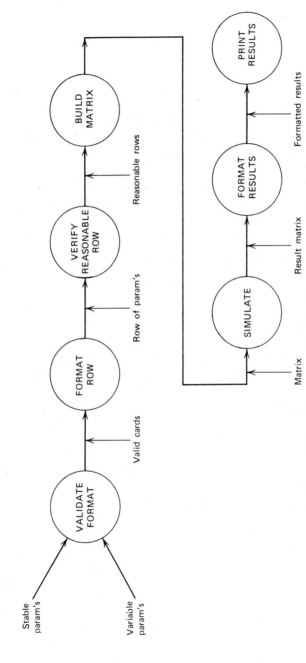

Figure 9.3 A data-flow diagram for "hotdog mix" program.

tion of meats that satisfies government and company constraints regarding maximum and minimum fat, protein, etc., for the hotdog. The basic mathematical approach is well established (linear programming). Modules are available that do linear programming—and this is the function of the "simulate" step. The data needs to be arranged in the proper format for the linear programming step, and the results formatted and printed.

Input to the program consists of stable parameters: the constraints on the content of the hotdog and the percentage content of different kinds of meat; and variable parameters: the current cost and available quantities of different kinds of meat. These parameters are read in and then validated. The result is valid cards. The valid cards are formatted into rows, resulting in rows of parameters. Each row is verified for reasonableness, for example, the constituents for any meat product should add up to 100 percent. Reasonable rows are built into a matrix (a two-dimensional array of data), which is input to the simulate step. The output of the linear programming process is a result matrix that indicates the optimal quantities of each type of meat to be used. This data is formatted and printed.

When drawing data-flow diagrams, make sure each circle contains a verb. Each process should do something *to* the data such as merge, select, transform, or rearrange. Also, identify the data which flows between the processes. Identification of the data will be important in the succeeding steps. The data into and out of a process should be consistent with what the process does, and vice versa.

Eliminate Minor Data Streams

Eliminate any minor streams of data from the diagram. Leave only major external streams of data that flow through the program. Error data streams are always minor. For the hotdog program, the invalid cards selected out by the validate format step is a minor stream of data. These minor streams would need to be shown in complete data-flow diagrams. But including them here makes it harder to find the top. If there is a question as to whether a stream of data is a minor one, eliminate it. In other words, err on the side of throwing away too many streams of data (but not *all* of them, of course). It is easy to add a stream of data to the chart once it gets built. But if it is not eliminated here, it will end up going through the top module, and several changes may be required to move it where it belongs—near the process that generates it.

Find the Top

This is done by identifying the last point where data can still be considered to be coming into the program and the first point where it can be considered to be going out (see Figure 9.4). Start where the data stream or streams go into the program. Step past each process, asking every time: Can this data still be viewed as data coming into the program? Identify the last point for which data can still be viewed as coming into the program.

In Figure 9.3, variable parameters and stable parameters are input to the program. Most people would identify valid cards as data still coming into the program. Also, rows of parameters and reasonable rows would seem to be data coming into the program. Matrix is the data finally assembled for the SIMULATE step. It can be viewed as input data. Result matrix, however, no longer seems to most people to be data coming in. If this is true, matrix is the last point for input data in Figure 9.3.

Do the same for output data, starting at the far end of the data-flow diagram and working leftwards. Step past each process asking: Can this still be viewed as data going out of the program? In Figure 9.3, formatted results and result matrix seem to be data going out of the program. However, matrix does not seem to be data going out of the program. Thus, result matrix may be identified to be the first point (left-to-right) where data seems to be output data.

Any process(es) left between the last point for input data and the first point for output data are called central transforms. Since many programs do not have central transforms, always be sure to inspect the last point for input data to see if it can *also* be identified as the first point for output data. Consider, for example, a program that reads cards and prints them. The process "read" results in cards which go to

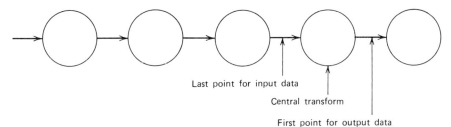

Figure 9.4   Last point for data in, first for data out.

the process "print." The last point for input data is cards, which is also the first point for output data. There is no transformation left between the input and output data points and, thus, no central transform.

This process helps identify what the designer considers to be the main purpose, or center, of the program. This becomes the initial top of the program. While identifying input and output points for data may seem subjective, experience shows that even inexperienced designers typically will differ by not more than one process in choosing these points.

Experience in making improvements to structure charts shows that identifying input points at or to the right of a point of convergence of any major streams of data results in fewer changes being needed later in the structured design process. Similarly, identifying output points at or to the left of diverging major streams of data seems to be the most valuable in arriving at solutions more quickly.

Define the Second Level

Define the modules for the second level on the basis of the points identified in the previous step. (The top module's function is already defined by the specifications for the program.) Call a module from the top module to get each *unique* stream of data that exists at the point identified as the last point for input data (Figure 9.5). For the hotdog mix example (in Figure 9.3), the module GET C is GET MATRIX, which returns the matrix to the top module. The top module's function is CALCULATE HOTDOG MIX.

Call a module from the top module for each stream of data that diverges at the first point for output data, whether the data streams are the same or different. Each module receives one of those streams.

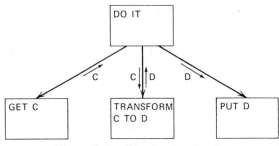

Figure 9.5   The top two levels.

However, the verbs for these module names are not as straightforward as those for the modules that get streams of data. Like that of the input modules, the function of these modules must represent the result of all the modules below it in the structure. In this case, though, that function is identified by determining what will ultimately happen to the data stream. These modules tend to have names such as PRODUCE REPORT ABC, PRODUCE PAYROLL CHECKS, STORE THE DATA.

For the hotdog mix example, there is one output stream of data and, thus, one module. The stream of data is the result matrix and the module's function is to produce the hotdog mix report.

The last part of step 4 is to include transform modules under the top module for any processes between the last point for input data and the first point for output data. The function or functions of these modules is to transform the data at the last point for input data into the data at the first point for output data. For the example in Figure 9.3, the central transform is SIMULATE. Its input data is the matrix and the output data is the result matrix.

Expand the Remaining Structure

Step 5 is to expand the structure below the modules resulting from step 4. Before doing this, discard the data-flow diagram. The processes shown in the data-flow diagram are not modules, and considering them as such will misdirect the initial structuring in some cases. For example, the printing of two distinct types of output should be shown as separate circles on the data-flow diagram. To use one circle would mean that the data has to be merged for printing to occur, which is not true. Since the process is the same, it is likely that a common module will end up being used. Another example of the difference between processes on data-flow diagrams and modules is the names. A process merging two streams of data will typically be named using "merge" (or some synonym) as a verb. However, the function of the module in which the merge takes place typically will be to *get* the resulting stream of data for its caller.

In order to expand GET C in Figure 9.5, identify the last transformation that occurred prior to having a C. Call the transform or transforms necessary to construct a C and call another module to get the data the transform needs for input (Figure 9.6). Then, expand the GET B module in a similar fashion.

For the hotdog example, this transform is BUILD MATRIX, which

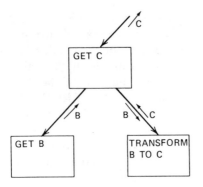

Figure 9.6   Modules below 'GET C'.

needs REASONABLE ROW as input. Thus, GET B becomes GET REASONABLE ROW.

PUT D, in Figure 9.5, is expanded in a similar fashion. Consider what the first transformation is which refines the data more toward its final form and call a transform, or transforms, from PUT D to do this. Then, call a module to put the resulting data stream (Figure 9.7). For the hotdog example, this transform is to format the results. Since there are no other transformations to be made in this case, PUT E is PRINT RESULTS.

Transforms may be single modules or may call other modules. Size and functionality are the most pertinent considerations for expanding the structure under transform modules. The better solutions should have functional names for each module. Evaluate alternative break-downs on the basis of binding and coupling. Look for common functions and functions potentially usable later. See also "Extracting a Module From Its Caller" in Chapter 7.

Complete the structure chart by adding the parameters necessary to allow it to meet the specifications of the program. For example, it typically is necessary to add ERROR and EOF to the parameter sets generated in step 3.

In practice it is tempting—and acceptable—to make improvements to the initial structure before it is complete. An effort should be made, though, to complete a structure early in this process so that the designer can be sure that "improvements" are not negatively impacting any other parts of the structure. See also "The Major Guidelines" section in Chapter 7.

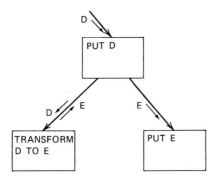

Figure 9.7   Modules below 'PUT D'.

Generating an Initial Chart for Patient Monitoring

In order to illustrate this procedure with another example, refer back to the specifications of the patient monitoring system in Chapter 8. The input data to this program is FACTORS. The factors are stored and checked. Unsafe factors are sent to the station. A data-flow diagram for this process is shown in Figure 9.8. Combining step 2 with step 1, the error messages about devices failing are not shown, as this is a minor stream of data. Step 3 is to find the last point for data in and the first for data out. Results of this step are shown in Figure 9.9, where the same point was identified as the last for data in and the first for data out.

Step 4 is to expand the top two levels. The top level is MONITOR PATIENTS. The single stream of data it must obtain at the "last point

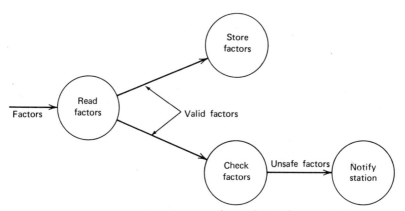

Figure 9.8   A data-flow diagram for MONITOR PATIENTS.

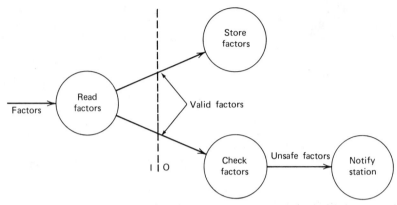

Figure 9.9   Last point for data in, first for data out.

for data in" is FACTORS. Thus, a module is called from MONITOR PATIENTS to obtain the factors.

The data diverges into two streams (at the first point for data out), and consequently two modules are needed. One reports unsafe factors, the other stores the factors (see Figure 9.10). Since the last point for data in is the same as the first for data out, there is no central transform. Referring back to the final chart in Chapter 8 for the MONITOR PATIENTS program, it may be seen that this initial chart can be expanded rather readily into something close to that final chart. Certainly, this start is much closer than the start indicated in Chapter 8.

Some Observations About This Process

Some observations are in order about this process. First, not much needs to be done regarding the extreme input or extreme output ends of the data-flow diagram, as they are not really used in the process. Secondly, if the designer can identify the top of the structure, the data-flow diagram need not be drawn at all. Data-flow diagrams are, however, useful in other phases of the implementation process, such as analysis. But as used here—to help the designer find the top of the structure— they need not be drawn if the designer can already pick the top of the structure. In fact, observation shows that most people find there is little need to draw these diagrams for more than the first few programs after learning the technique. This is more a description of a thinking process

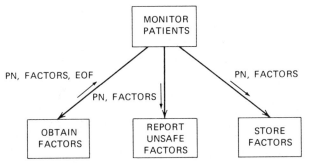

Figure 9.10   The top two levels for "patient monitoring."

to use in finding the top of a program than of an actual mechanical process where the diagram must be drawn.

Summary

Any technique for drawing an initial structure that satisfies the specifications is acceptable. The final result can be derived from any such initial structure. The most useful initial structure to consider is the common one, with its variations, shown in Figure 9.1, since most business programs result in this structure. The top module can be identified immediately: its function is that specified by the requirements for the program. In order to find the second level, a five-step heuristic procedure can be followed.

Step 1 is to draw a data-flow diagram for the major streams of data flowing through the program. Step 2 is to identify and eliminate any minor streams of data that were drawn, and all error streams of data are minor streams.

Step 3 is to identify the point farthest into the data-flow diagram where data can still be viewed as coming in, and to find the first point where data can be viewed as going out. This is done by starting at the left side of the data-flow diagram and stepping rightwards, process by process, until the data can no longer be considered as data coming into the program. While any point is usable, the most useful point for finding the top level typically is either at or to the right of converging streams of data. Then, do the same for output data, stepping process by process from the right end of the diagram leftwards until data can no longer be considered data going out. The last point for data coming in and the first for data going out are often the same. If they are not, any processes in between are identified as central transforms.

Step 4 is to expand the second level of the structure on the basis of the preceding points. Call a module from the top mode to return each *unique* stream of data occurring at the point identified as the last point for data coming in. Call a module that receives *each* stream of data (whether unique or not) that diverges at the point identified as the first point for data going out. Add modules to do any transforms located between the points for data in and data out. The major data items going in and out of each of these modules are the same as on the data-flow diagram.

Step 5 is to expand the lower levels. First, throw the data-flow diagram away. Next, expand modules that get streams of data by identifying the last transformation needed to produce that data, and by getting input for that transformation. Similarly, modules that receive a stream of data should call a module to do the first transformation of the data, and then "put" the resulting data. Transform modules are expanded primarily on the basis of functionality and size.

10
A Design Example

In order to illustrate the entire process of structured design, a program will be taken through all steps from specifications through to a final structure. The program is one a brokerage house might use to print histograms (bar charts—see Figure 10.1) of how much of each type of stock is owned by the customers of each broker. The program updates the tape master file with any pending transactions so that the histograms will reflect the latest data. It also produces a composite histogram for the entire company.

The specifications for this program are not functionally bound. It is not suggested that such multifunction programs be designed. The reason such a program is being used as an example is that the designer may not always have the luxury of designing programs whose specifications are functionally bound. Moreover, single-function programs are a subset of multifunction programs, as will be illustrated later in the chapter.

```
                      BROKER J. K. SMITH
                    THOUSANDS OF SHARES

              5K    10K   15K   20K   25K   30K   35K   40K   45K   50K
              V     V     V     V     V     V     V     V     V     V
STOCK NAME  A:  XXXXXXX
STOCK NAME  B:  XXX
STOCK NAME  C:  XXXXXXXXXXXXXXXXX
```

Figure 10.1 A broker histogram.

The specifications for this program have been intentionally limited so that attention can be focused on the technique rather than on a complex set of specifications. The technique and approach are the same when the specifications are complex—there are just *more* of them to be considered. The details for the specifications follow.

The master file is in order by customer name within broker. The master record contains the customer ID, the customer name, the broker name, and stock types (ID) and quantities (QTY) owned by the customer (Figure 10.2). The customer ID is a coded representation of the customer's name and the broker's name (such that customer ID order is the same order as customer name within broker).

A daily transaction file is in chronological order within customer name within broker. Transaction records all contain the transaction type, customer ID, broker name, and customer name. A change transaction can change a field or one or more of the stock amounts. Other transactions can add a customer (create a new master record) or delete a customer. Assume that customers are only allowed to sell stock they already have, that is, no negative quantities will occur in the master record.

Transactions are to be checked to make sure that the customer ID is correct, based on the broker name and customer name from the same record. Write an error message for new customer transactions that have a matching master record and for all other transactions that have no matching master record. Assume that no other errors can occur. The program is also to write any deleted master records to an audit file. Assume that the scaling can be the same for all histograms. Stocks can appear in any order within the histograms. There will not be more than 2000 different stocks in a histogram. The program should do something reasonable with stock ID's for which it has no stock name. Put a heading only at the top of each histogram and then print continuously until that histogram is complete.

The Data Flow Diagram

The first step (as described in Chapter 9) is to draw a data-flow diagram for the program (either literally or mentally). The data into the

'stock list'

CUST ID, BROKER NAME, CUST NAME,. . . COUNT, ID, QTY, ID, QTY, ID, QTY,. . .

Figure 10.2 Master record (variable length).

program are TRANSACTIONS and MASTER RECORDS. TRANSACTIONS are to be checked to see that the customer ID is correct. The resulting CHECKED TRANSACTIONS are needed to update the MASTER RECORDS (see Figure 10.3). DELETED MASTERS are to be written out to a log file. NEW MASTERS (i.e., the records for what will be the new master file) have to be written out to a new master file. NEW MASTERS are also needed as input to an accumulation process that accumulates BROKER TOTALS. The resulting BROKER TOTALS have to be converted to strings of X's of the appropriate length to produce histogram LINES. The histogram LINES can then be printed.

Figure 10.3 is not complete. It is still necessary to add the process for producing the composite histogram for the entire brokerage company. The accumulation process is basically the same as for accumulating BROKER TOTALS. The input for the accumulation, though, can be either NEW MASTERS or BROKER TOTALS, since either will generate the correct results. Since most people pick BROKER TOTALS, the problem will proceed on that basis. BROKER TOTALS are accumulated to produce COMPANY TOTALS. These are converted to histogram LINES, which are printed (see Figure 10.4).

Notice that it would be incorrect to send COMPANY TOTALS into the previous PRODUCE HISTOGRAM LINES. To do so would imply that COMPANY TOTALS *and* BROKER TOTALS are both used to produce histogram LINES, which is not correct. The processes (circles) on data-flow diagrams are *not* modules (even though two similar processes may end up being implemented by the same module).

Step 2 is to eliminate minor streams of data. The DELETED MASTERS do not seem to be a primary output of this program, so that stream will be eliminated. The NEW MASTERS being written to the new master file seem to be one of the main outputs, so that stream of data will be kept.

Step 3 is to find the input and output points for the data coming in and going out, respectively. This step is subjective. There are other valid opinions, which result in other initial charts. It might be interesting to note your opinion and compare it to the top two levels of the *final* solution later. TRANSACTIONS and MASTER RECORDS are certainly data coming into the program. CHECKED TRANSACTIONS also seems like data coming into the program. NEW MASTERS can be viewed as data coming into the program. However, BROKER TOTALS do not seem to be data coming into the program. So the last

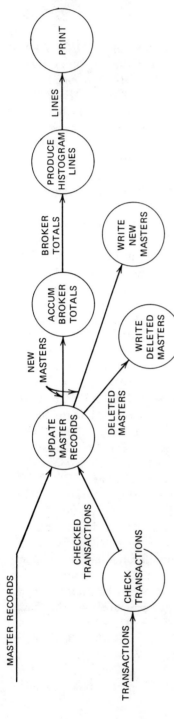

Figure 10.3 A partial data-flow diagram.

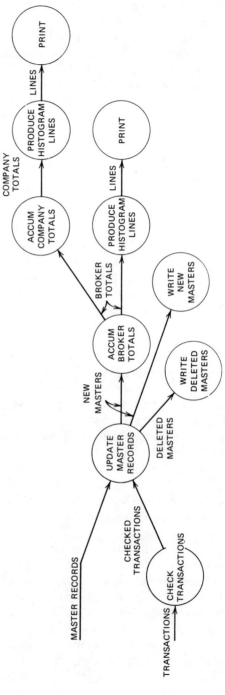

Figure 10.4 A complete data-flow diagram.

154

point where data is identified as still coming into the program is as shown in Figure 10.5.

LINES is certainly data going out of the program. COMPANY TOTALS and then BROKER TOTALS also look like data going out of the program. NEW MASTERS, however, do not look like data going out of the program (except in the leg going to WRITE NEW MASTERS). With this choice, the output points are as in Figure 10.6.

The Top Two Levels

Based on the choices made above (and shown in Figure 10.6), the top two levels of the structure can be drawn as explained in "Define the Second Level" in Chapter 9. The top module is STOCK PROFILE. (It really should be PRODUCE BROKER AND COMPANY HISTOGRAMS AND UPDATE THE MASTER FILE, but STOCK PROFILE will do for now for illustrative purposes.) At the input point there is one unique stream of data: NEW MASTERS. Thus one module is called from the top module, which will return a new master record to its caller. Its name is GET NEW MASTER.

There are three streams of data (unique or not) at the output point(s) in Figure 10.6. Thus, three modules that each dispose of a stream of data are called from the top module. Their names should represent what will happen from that point to the right, using that stream of data. Thus they are named PUT NEW MASTER, PRODUCE BROKER HISTOGRAM, and PRODUCE COMPANY HISTOGRAM. The result so far is shown in Figure 10.7.

There is one process between the input and output points. This becomes the central transform: ACCUMULATE BROKER TOTALS (ACCUM. BR. TOTS). With this added as a module, the top two levels are as shown in Figure 10.8.

The parameters for the top two levels have been generally determined from the data-flow diagram. However, additional parameters are necessary in order to make it work. An EOF is needed with NEW MASTER from the module GET NEW MASTER. An EOF also needs to be passed along with NEW MASTER to the modules PUT NEW MASTER and PRODUCE COMPANY HISTORGRAM. (The first uses it to close the file, the second uses it to know when to produce the composite histogram.) Broker totals (BR. TOTS) are contained within the module STOCK PROFILE. Since this parameter is not a single data element, its format should be detailed. A possible format for BR. TOTS could be as shown in Figure 10.9. COUNT indicates how many

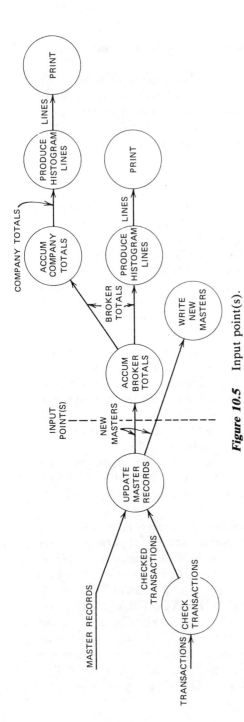

Figure 10.5 Input point(s).

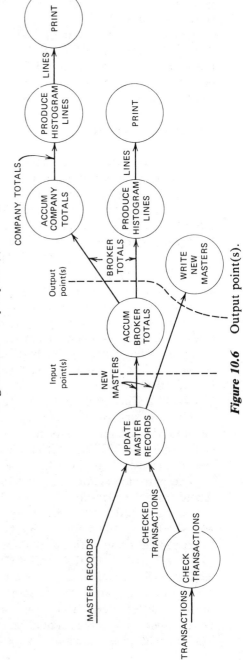

Figure 10.6 Output point(s).

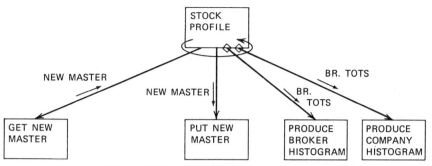

Figure 10.7 Part of the top two levels.

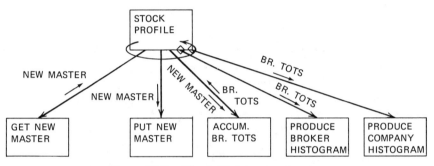

Figure 10.8 The initial top two levels.

stock ID/quantity pairs are currently in the table. BR. TOTS are passed to ACCUM. BR. TOTS with a new master record. ACCUM. BR. TOTS updates the accumulating totals with the stocks in the master record and passes them back. Since data passes each way, BR. TOTS is shown both going to, and being returned from, the module ACCUM. BR. TOTS. PRODUCE BROKER HISTOGRAM also needs the broker name to print on the first line of the broker histogram. See Figure 10.10.

Expansion of the Structure Below

The next step is to stop using the data-flow diagram and continue to expand the structure. The structure will be expanded below GET NEW MASTER first. The last transformation(s) that occur before getting a new master are to update the master record. Since there are three types

COUNT	
ID	QTY
ID	QTY
ID	QTY

Figure 10.9 BROKER TOTALS parameter.

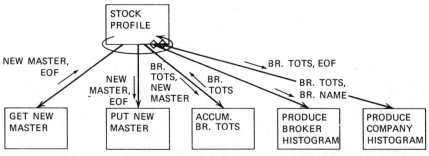

Figure 10.10 Necessary parameters added to top levels.

of update transactions—change, add, and delete—three transaction modules seem appropriate. These are CHANGE MASTER, CREATE NEW MASTER, and LOG DELETED MASTER (the delete is trivial, but the latter module logs it to the audit file). GET NEW MASTER also calls modules to get data for those transforms—namely, GET MASTER and GET TRANS. Since, however, the specifications require transactions to be validated (the customer ID must be correct, based on the broker name and customer name within the transaction record), the name of the latter module should be GET VALID TRANS (Figure 10.11). The data returned from GET MASTER is a master record and MEOF (master end of file). The data returned from GET VALID TRANS is a transaction and TEOF (transaction end of file).

The data for CHANGE MASTER is a change transaction and

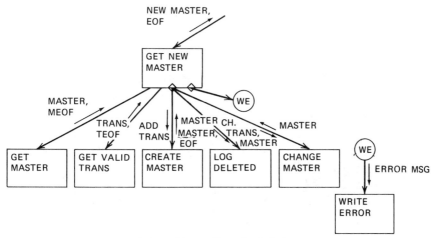

Figure 10.11 Expanding the left leg.

master record in, and the changed master returned. The data for CREATE MASTER is an add transaction in and a new master returned. The data to LOG DELETED MASTER is master record and EOF.

GET VALID TRANS calls the modules VALIDATE TRANS and READ TRANS. The data for VALIDATE TRANS is the transaction in and a valid-switch (VALIDSW) returned. (The SW on VALIDSW is for "switch" and implies its binary nature, which improves the observability.) The data for READ TRANS is the transaction and TEOF, both returned. VALIDATE TRANS calls WRITE ERROR if the transaction ID is not valid. Since this leg now solves its part of the specifications, this part of the initial structure chart is done. Once the whole structure chart is complete, this part can be reviewed to see if any improvements can be made. The chart is now as shown in Figure 10.12.

ACCUM. BR. TOTS does not seem to need to call any other modules, and neither does PUT NEW MASTER.

The next thing to be expanded is PRODUCE BROKER HISTO-GRAM. PRODUCE BROKER HISTOGRAM calls GET STOCK NAME. It passes the stock ID and gets back the expanded stock name. If the stock name is not available, the most desirable thing would seem to be to print the stock ID. If so, by having GET STOCK NAME pass back the stock ID when a name is not available, it will not be necessary for an error parameter to be returned (nor will PRODUCE BROKER

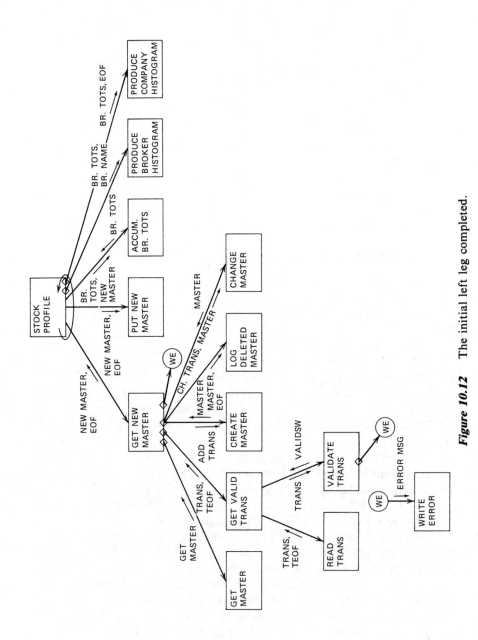

Figure 10.12 The initial left leg completed.

HISTOGRAM need to check the error parameter). PRODUCE BRO-
KER HISTOGRAM then calls PRINT, passing a line to be printed.
The structure chart is now as shown in Figure 10.13.

PRODUCE COMPANY HISTOGRAM will be expanded next. It
needs to accumulate company totals, so it calls a module ACCUM. CO.
TOTS. ACCUM. CO. TOTS takes the broker totals and the accumulating company totals (CO. TOTS) as input and returns the updated
company totals. The CO. TOTS table can be in the same format as BR.
TOTS (Figure 10.9). If PRODUCE COMPANY HISTOGRAM then
calls PRODUCE BROKER HISTOGRAM, passing the *company*
totals and the brokerage *company* name, the latter module will produce
a company histogram! But the name of the latter module should now be
something like PUT HISTOGRAM. The whole structure is now as in
Figure 10.14. This is a complete initial structure chart. The modules are
all passed sufficient information for the specifications to be completely
implemented.

Improvements to the Structure

GET NEW MASTER does the match and update logic for updating
the master file. Its name is based on what happens between when it is
called and when it returns—from its caller's point of view. (See "Names
for Modules" in Chapter 5.) Although internally it updates the master
record, UPDATE MASTER is not a good name for it. It is called by
STOCK PROFILE to get a new master. As far as STOCK PROFILE
is concerned, it could be getting a new master by reading it off a new
master file. The name UPDATE MASTER implies a transform module
like CHANGE MASTER in Figure 10.14, which is *passed* the record
to be updated by its caller. Although UPDATE MASTER FILE might
be a good name for the top module of a program that updates the entire
master file before returning (to the operating system), GET NEW
MASTER is a much more descriptive name for this module in this
structure.

GET NEW MASTER is, however, fairly complicated. It would help
if a module could be extracted from it to simplify it. One possibility
seems to be a module UPDATE MASTER as shown in Figure 10.15.
UPDATE MASTER is passed the transaction and the master record
and returns a new master. However, in order for UPDATE MASTER
to do its job properly, it also needs MEOF and TEOF. Further, since
there will not always be a new master returned to GET NEW MAS-
TER (e.g. on a delete transaction) it is necessary to return a MASTER-

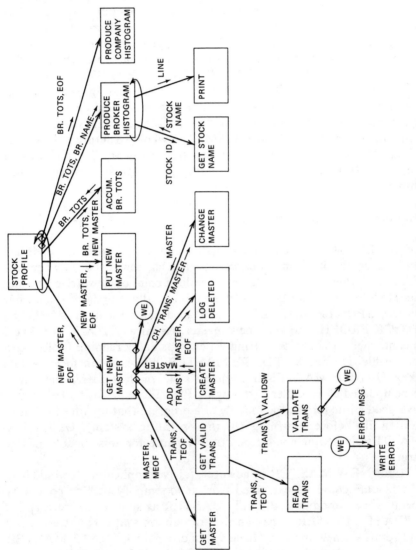

Figure 10.13 Expanding the right side.

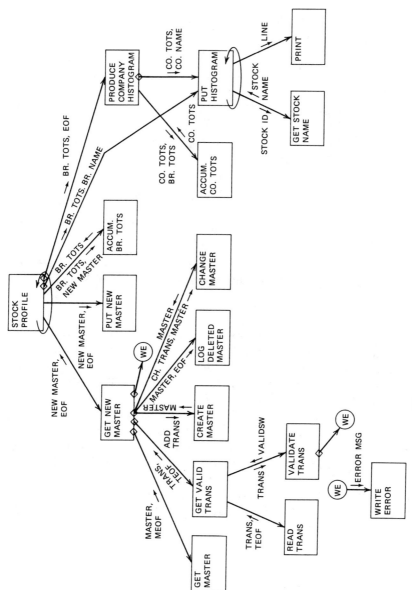

Figure 10.14 A complete initial chart.

163

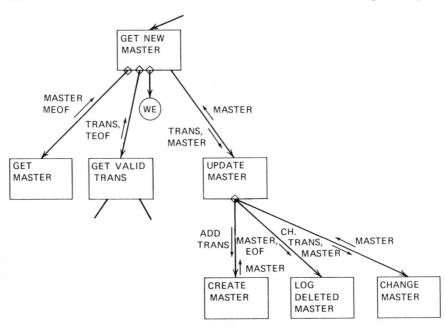

Figure 10.15   An attempt to simplify GET NEW MASTER.

SWITCH to indicate whether or not there is a new master being returned. Even with this, though, GET NEW MASTER will not know whether it is time to get a transaction or to get a new master (e.g., there may be another transaction for the same master). The only way it could know is if it duplicates the logic in UPDATE MASTER. But this is exactly the logic that UPDATE MASTER is supposed to remove from GET NEW MASTER. Even if it were duplicated, adding extra parameters from UPDATE MASTER to GET NEW MASTER would be justified in order to eliminate this duplicate function. (See "Avoid Duplicating Functions" in Chapter 7.) Thus, the simplest alternative is to pass a GET-TRANS-SWITCH and a GET-MASTER-SWITCH from UPDATE MASTER to GET NEW MASTER. Now UPDATE MASTER has sufficient parameters to work properly without functions being duplicated within GET NEW MASTER (Figure 10.16).

It is not an improvement to combine the three return switches (NEW-MASTER-SWITCH, GET-TRANS-SWITCH, and GET-MASTER-SWITCH) into one or two switches. The same data is still passed, but the observability is lower. Thus the coupling is increased.

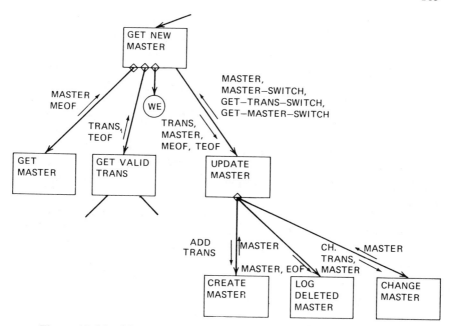

Figure 10.16 Necessary parameters added to UPDATE MASTER.

Admittedly, MASTER-SWITCH could be inferred from GET-TRANS-SWITCH and GET-MASTER-SWITCH both being off. Also, one switch could be defined with multiple states that indicate whether to get a transaction or a master. All of this assumes that there will never be a need to set multiple switches at the same time. But it is in fact quite reasonable to get a transaction and get a master at the same time (e.g., after a delete transaction). Most important, though, faced with the options of three switches or fewer switches for three distinct conditions, choose the alternative that *allows* all possibilities in the future—whether or not it seems today that those combinations could ever exist. It costs only a very small amount of memory—it does not even require extra conditional branches, since all the conditions must be tested anyway. Moreover, the interface is clearer with three binary switches rather than with two or one multistate switches. With multistate switches, anyone who wants to understand the interface must look further into documentation and/or code in order to understand what the conditions mean—in order to know how to call the module.

If UPDATE MASTER knows enough to tell GET NEW MASTER

when it needs a transaction record (via GET-TRANS-SWITCH), then it is simpler if UPDATE MASTER calls GET VALID TRANS itself. This eliminates the GET-TRANS-SWITCH, the transaction, and TEOF from the interface to UPDATE MASTER, which reduces the coupling. Similarly, if UPDATE MASTER knows enough to tell GET NEW MASTER when to get a master record (via GET-MASTER-SWITCH), then it is simpler if UPDATE MASTER calls GET MASTER itself. This eliminates the GET-MASTER-SWITCH, the master record, and MEOF from the interface to UPDATE MASTER. However, UPDATE MASTER must now return EOF to GET NEW MASTER. UPDATE MASTER also has to be the one now to call WRITE ERROR. See Figure 10.17.

Now UPDATE MASTER needs to return to GET NEW MASTER only when there is a valid new master record. Thus, the MASTER-SWITCH can be eliminated. But GET NEW MASTER now does nothing but pass parameters to and from UPDATE MASTER. Thus it can be eliminated. Moreover, the function of UPDATE MASTER is no

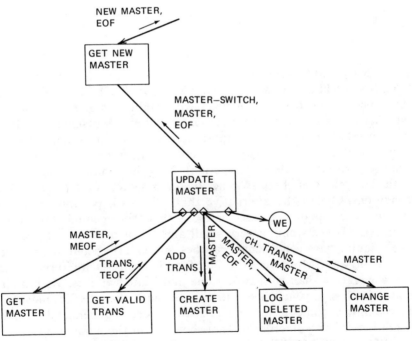

Figure 10.17 Improving the proposed change.

longer a transform type of function, as is implied by the name
UPDATE MASTER. The function is to get a new master record, thus
its name should be GET NEW MASTER. The structure is again as in
Figure 10.14.

Although an attempt was made to pull some function out of GET
NEW MASTER, successive improvements to the proposed change
resulted in the original structure. If improvements to a proposed change
produce the original structure, then it follows that the original structure
was better than the proposed change. Why was it that the change did
not work? The logic for getting a new master and getting a transaction
is intimately related to the mix and match logic for doing the update.
Any attempt to separate these two highly related pieces into two
separate modules results in a high degree of coupling between the two
modules. In order to eliminate the high coupling, the separate pieces
have to be brought together again. This was done piece by piece as
improvements were made to eliminate the control switches.

GET NEW MASTER does call six other modules. In "Modules
That Call More Than Three to Five Others," in Chapter 7, it is
suggested that such modules should be checked for possible problems.
But it also points out there that a case where a module can validly call
more than three to five others is for the transaction structure (described
in "Standard Forms" in Chapter 7). GET NEW MASTER is a transaction structure: in GET NEW MASTER there are three possible
transaction types and a multiway decision as to which module to call.
Thus the number of modules called by GET NEW MASTER turns out
not to be signaling a problem.

Next, consider the VALIDATE TRANS module in Figure 10.14.
The coupling for this module can be reduced by passing only the
customer ID, customer name, and broker name (instead of passing the
entire transaction). The coupling can be reduced even further by passing the broker name and customer name down and passing the customer
ID back. This eliminates the valid-switch. But a better name for *this*
module is GEN. CUST. ID (generate customer ID). This change is
shown in Figure 10.18. Notice that the usability of this module has been
increased. Moreover, the usability increased when the parameters
decreased! This is an example of what was referred to in Chapter 7 in
the section "Allow for Flexibility." Flexibility typically goes up when
parameters are *decreased* rather than when they are *increased*—
although the temptation is usually to try to increase flexibility by
adding parameters. The check of whether the customer ID on the
transaction is correct is now being done in GET VALID TRANS. Thus,

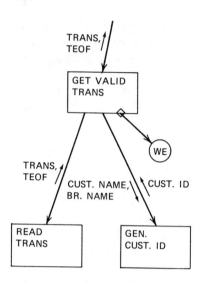

Figure 10.18 Decreased coupling for GEN CUST ID.

the error message for invalid transactions will have to be issued from GET VALID TRANS. This also agrees with the suggestion in "Elements of a Functional Module" in Chapter 7. Error messages issued on the basis of a binary error parameter returned by a module are often more useful and clearer when issued from the immediate caller—which is usually testing the error parameter anyway.

Since no other improvements are seen for this part of the structure, attention will be turned to the middle (see Figure 10.14). There seems to be a lot of similarity between ACCUM. BR. TOTS and ACCUM. CO. TOTS, although the two modules are not exactly the same. A procedure described in "Avoid Duplicating Functions" in Chapter 7 can be used here: first look for the common part and extract it in a module below the two similar modules.

But first, the coupling to ACCUM. BR. TOTS can be reduced. The only thing that really needs to be passed to it out of the master record is the stock list portion (see Figure 10.2: the part of the record that has a COUNT and then a number of ID, QTY pairs). This improvement is shown in Figure 10.19. Now it is not necessary to extract the module below the two similar modules because they are no longer different. The format of the stock list portion of the record is exactly the same as that specified for BROKER TOTALS, a COUNT followed by ID, QTY, ID, QTY . . . (compare Figures 10.2 and 10.9). So the parameters for ACCUM. BR. TOTS have exactly the same format as those for

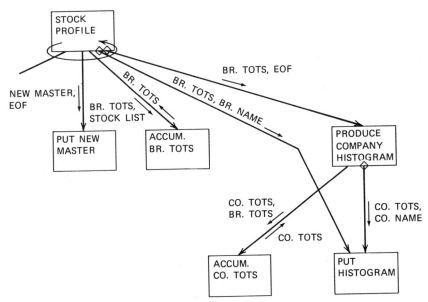

Figure 10.19   Reduced coupling for ACCUM. BR. TOTS.

ACCUM. CO. TOTS. Thus a single module, ACCUM. STOCK TOTALS, can be called from both places with the current parameters as in Figure 10.20.

The top module is involved in the details of producing a report. It has field definitions for the master record so that it can pass the stock list. It contains the broker total table and it detects broker breaks (change of broker name). It is not as functionally bound as it could be, since its function should only be to make sure the program runs and accomplishes its objective(s). The report-related function can be pulled out into a module PRODUCE BROKER HISTOGRAM, as shown in Figure 10.21. STOCK PROFILE passes this module the master record and EOF. However, STOCK PROFILE no longer has the broker totals to pass to PRODUCE COMPANY HISTOGRAM, so the latter module is passed the NEW MASTER. NEW MASTER is also sufficient to calculate COMPANY TOTALS accurately. PRODUCE COMPANY HISTOGRAM also passes the STOCK LIST to ACCUM. CO. TOTS, instead of passing BR. TOTS. Any performance implications of this change should be ignored if the simplest solution is to be reached. Only the simplest solution should be optimized for performance, because it

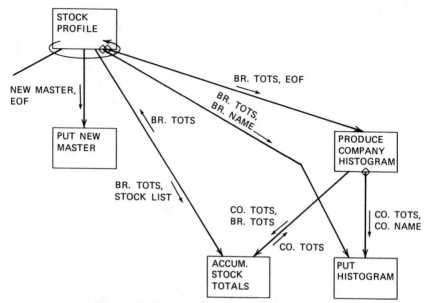

Figure 10.20 Duplicate function eliminated.

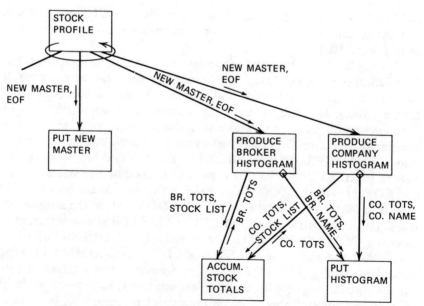

Figure 10.21 Improved binding for STOCK PROFILE.

will be the easiest to optimize (if it even still needs to be optimized, which it often does not).

The name field can be eliminated from the interface to PUT HIS-TOGRAM in Figure 10.21 by having the PRODUCE BROKER HIS-TOGRAM and PRODUCE COMPANY HISTOGRAM modules call PRINT directly to print the line that has the broker name or company name on it (reference Figure 10.1). This reduces the coupling to PUT HISTOGRAM. Notice that the extra call to PRINT is not a trade-off for the reduced coupling, since the extra call has no effect on coupling. The coupling of PRINT is unchanged; it still uses the same parameters. How many callers there are has no bearing on coupling (see in Chapter 7, "The Presence or Absence of a Call Does Not Affect Coupling"). This part of the structure is shown in Figure 10.22. The total structure is now as shown in Figure 10.23.

One more function is duplicated within the structure. The reader may find it interesting to try to identify the duplicate function in Figure 10.23 before reading further.

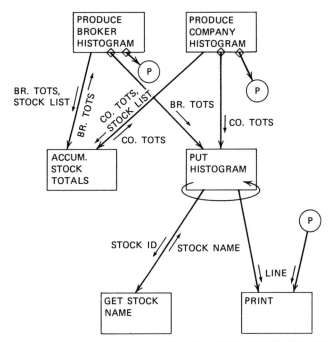

Figure 10.22 Reduced coupling for PUT HISTOGRAM.

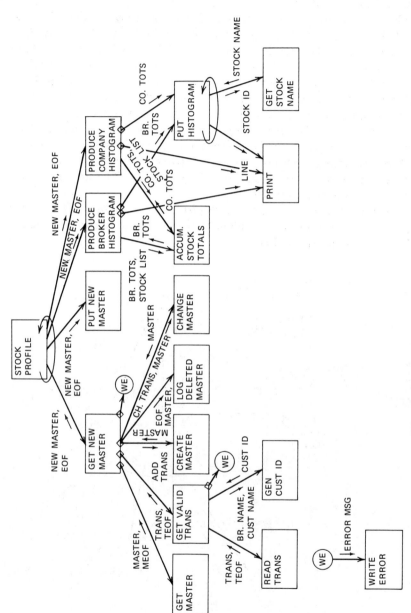

Figure 10.23 An almost complete chart.

172

A way to accumulate individual quantities for both the broker totals and the company totals is to take each new stock ID, QTY pair and look for an existing match in the table. If a match is found, the new quantity is added into the table quantity. Otherwise, the new ID, QTY pair is added to the end of the table and the COUNT is increased by one. The same process would also adjust the quantities in the master record based on ID, QTY pairs in a change transaction. Thus there is some duplicate function between ACCUM. STOCK TOTALS and CHANGE MASTER.

In examining what portion is common, it appears that the common portion is *all* of ACCUM. STOCK TOTALS. However, CHANGE MASTER needs a facility not currently in ACCUM. STOCK TOTALS. The fact that transactions may decrement will be all right, since those counts will be negative quantities that will add without a problem. If quantities go to zero, however, it presumably is desirable to compress the variable-length string of ID, QTY pairs in the master record so that the pair with the quantity of zero is eliminated. Thus, to use ACCUM. STOCK TOTALS would require that the module be written in a slightly more complex fashion. If this "increase" in complexity seems in any way questionable, consider it a different way. Write the function that solves what CHANGE MASTER needs *first*. It needs to be written at some point anyway. Once it is written, there is *no* justification for writing another module that does less. This module will already do the job needed by the right hand leg of the structure. The structure is now as shown in Figure 10.24.

It may be thought that the coupling could be reduced by passing just the stock list to the produce histogram modules. But this is not the case. One reason is that PRODUCE BROKER HISTOGRAM also needs to be passed the broker name (for the title on the histogram). In addition, MASTER RECORD is a single parameter to STOCK PROFILE anyway. It is no more complicated for STOCK PROFILE to handle than if it were a single data item. Thus the coupling would go up if STOCK PROFILE tried to pass fields instead of a record because two data items would be passed instead of one.

It may be useful to examine how the (slightly) better coupling of passing the master record implies a (slightly) reduced complexity. This examination is not meant to imply that, when doing designs, the designer must also examine alternatives which exhibit better binding or coupling in order to identify how and why the reduced complexity or increased flexibility is achieved. It is hoped that this book will provide enough confidence in binding and coupling so that this extra step can be

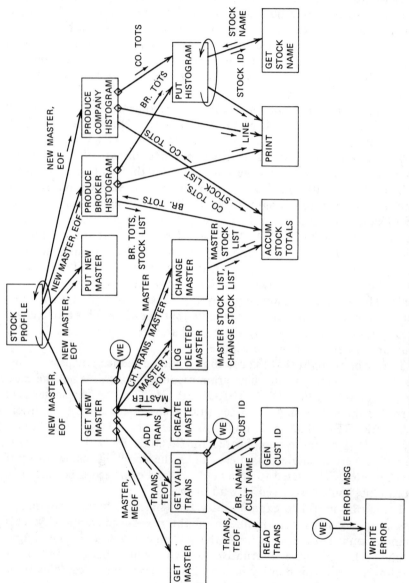

Figure 10.24   A final structure chart.

eliminated during actual designs. If STOCK PROFILE breaks up the fields needed by PRODUCE BROKER HISTOGRAM, then it gets involved in specifications for the report. If, in the future, PRODUCE BROKER HISTOGRAM needs additional fields in order to do its job, then two modules have to be changed, STOCK PROFILE and PRO-DUCE BROKER HISTOGRAM. While in this program the field definitions are needed in two modules, PRODUCE BROKER HISTO-GRAM and PRODUCE COMPANY HISTOGRAM, note that the second is basically a copy of the first anyway. Moreover, the broker name only needs to be defined in PRODUCE BROKER HISTO-GRAM, and the format of the stock list is only defined within ACCUM. STOCK TOTALS. Thus, only the starting location of the stock list within the master record is duplicated, and these two occur-rences would be in different programs if the specifications had not required multiple functions for this program.

The module ACCUM. STOCK TOTALS can be used by CHANGE MASTER if the transaction record is in the same format as the master record. What if such is not the case, for example, if there is no COUNT field and only one ID, QTY is on the change record? It still is easy to eliminate the duplicate function. All that is needed is for CHANGE MASTER to move the ID, QTY pair to an area that is preceded by a count of 1 and then to call ACCUM. STOCK TOTALS.

If the specifications had only allowed one change per transaction, it might even be worthwhile to ask if the user would like to have multiple changes per transaction. Note that it is *easier* to handle the increased function than it is to handle the more restrictive function! This is not unusual when doing structured design. When functions are duplicated within the same program (as typically happens in monolithic solutions), often the specifications require more versatility in one of the occur-rences than in the others. When the common function is identified and extracted into a separately compiled module so it can be called from the multiple places, it can provide the wider versatility for each of those callers.

The solution in Figure 10.24 has been considered by many people. Improvements have been made to earlier solutions. The author wel-comes other suggestions for further improvements for this structure.

Consider Possible Changes

Consider some possible changes for this program. If the final solution has eliminated all the binding and coupling problems, it should be changeable, thus reasonable changes should be easy to implement. The specifications for this program were reduced drastically in order to keep this illustrative example simple. Thus some of these changes may seem to be almost necessary specifications (rather than "changes"). One of these "necessary" specifications is automatic scaling. With any reasonable number of brokers, either the company histogram will go off the chart or the broker histograms will be so small that variations can not be seen. In the solution in Figure 10.24, only one module, PUT HISTO-GRAM, needs to be changed in order to have automatic scaling. It looks at the totals matrix and determines an appropriate scaling factor based on the largest quantity found within the matrix.

Another possible change is to print the three-letter stock ID in front of the stock name for each line of the histogram. For this change, only GET STOCK NAME needs to be changed. The returned character string is changed to have the three-letter stock ID in front of the stock name. Another change which might now be desirable is to have the stocks charted in alphabetical order by stock ID. While the temptation here might be to sort the totals before calling PUT HISTOGRAM, there is an interesting alternative. The stock ID's will be in order if ACCUM. STOCK TOTALS simply inserts new stocks in their respective alphabetical positions within the table (rather than adding them to the end of the table). This also results in the stocks within the master record being in alphabetical order. This could be a significant advantage if the master records are ever to be reviewed on-line. Stock records that need more than one screen in order to be displayed will be difficult to search visually if they are not in alphabetical order. The user may find this change to be very advantageous, and since it is quite simple, it might well be justified.

This last change also presents an opportunity for a performance trade-off. (Now that the design is at the end, it is an appropriate time to look for performance trade-offs.) With the stock ID's in alphabetical order, there is an opportunity for ACCUM. STOCK TOTALS to do a binary search. With the quantity of stocks approaching 1000 to 2000, the performance benefit of doing a binary search over a serial search is dramatic. For 1000 records, a serial search averages 500 compares. For a binary search the maximum is 10, with the average being 5. The performance advantage is tremendous. The complexity increase is only slight, especially in COBOL, where there is a verb to do a binary search. In fact, the performance gains are so substantial that this single change probably saves more in performance than the overhead of all of the calls in the entire structure. It also gains back the performance lost when the change was made from having PRODUCE COMPANY HISTO-GRAM accumulate company totals from each master rather than from the broker totals. This is an example of why it is important to find the simplest solution first, and then (if optimization is ever needed) look for ways to get the most performance for the least increase in complexity.

Consider what has to change if the master file is on a direct access device, in other words only changed, added, or deleted records have to be written back to the file. The structure does not need to be changed, but a status parameter needs to be passed along with NEW MASTER. The status parameter indicates whether the master is a changed, added, or deleted master. It is needed so PUT NEW MASTER can execute the correct "write" operation. Because of the multiple functions specified for STOCK PROFILE, the top module also needs to check this status parameter in order to know which records to pass along to PRODUCE BROKER HISTOGRAM and to PRODUCE COMPANY HISTO-GRAM. In a program which only updates the master file (as will be discussed below) GET NEW MASTER would not have to pass back existing unchanged masters (and could be named GET CHANGED MASTER).

Alternatives Relative to the Data-Flow Diagram

Consider the results of some alternative choices on the data-flow diagram. If the input point is picked at point 1 in Figure 10.25, the left side of the top two levels will be as in Figure 10.26. This result has almost exactly the same problems as those described earlier relative to the module UPDATE MASTER (see Figures 10.15, 10.16, and 10.17). In order to make the structure work, function has to be duplicated or control has to be passed. Added control parameters can then be eliminated if UPDATE MASTER calls GET MASTER and GET VALID TRANS itself. But then its name should be GET NEW MASTER rather than the transformlike name UPDATE MASTER. The resulting structure would be as was shown in Figure 10.24.

If the output point(s) are chosen at point 2 in Figure 10.25, then the top two levels of the structure are as in Figure 10.27. The same structure results as in Figure 10.24, except that where Figure 10.24 has two modules, PRODUCE BROKER HISTOGRAM and PRODUCE COMPANY HISTOGRAM, Figure 10.27 has only one module, PRO-DUCE HISTOGRAMS. However, one of these alternatives is an improvement over the other. They can be evaluated on the basis of the

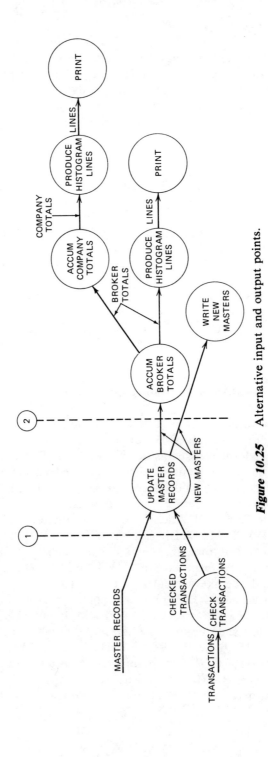

Figure 10.25   Alternative input and output points.

178

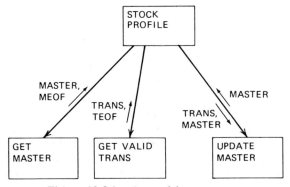

Figure 10.26 A resulting structure.

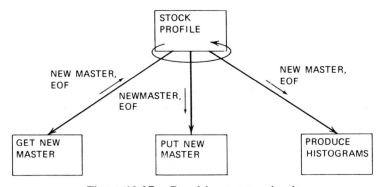

Figure 10.27 Resulting top two levels.

concepts of binding and coupling, and the guidelines and tips in Chapter 7.

PRODUCE HISTOGRAMS is not functionally bound. The tests for functional binding suggested in Chapter 5 in the section "Identifying Functional Binding" indicate that the object of the verb in the name of a module must be specific. Here, "histograms" is plural, and in fact this module does produce two different (even though similar) histograms. Compare this to the structure in Figure 10.24 where these two functions are separate. Binding considerations say that the separate function alternative is preferable. This is sufficient to justify this alternative as an improvement.

It may be helpful, however, to investigate in what ways the complexity is reduced and changeability is enhanced in the separate function alternative (as predicted by the improved binding). One issue is which is easier to implement, PRODUCE BROKER HISTOGRAM plus PRODUCE COMPANY HISTOGRAM, or PRODUCE HISTOGRAMS. Although the difference may be small—because of the simple specifications here – the *direction* of the difference is the significant thing to note. It may not be clear whether PRODUCE HISTOGRAMS is easier to implement than the two modules, so consider it in two steps. First, compare PRODUCE HISTOGRAMS to PRODUCE BROKER HISTOGRAM. The latter is easier to implement. PRODUCE HISTOGRAMS has the same code in it as PRODUCE BROKER HISTOGRAM, but PRODUCE HISTOGRAMS has to *repeat* the code to produce the company histogram. (It cannot use the same code twice because it is dealing with different quantity matrices and has different titles for the top of the histograms.) Secondly, given PRODUCE BROKER HISTOGRAM, it is trivial to create the module PRODUCE COMPANY HISTOGRAM. Simply copy the source for PRODUCE BROKER HISTOGRAM, rename it, and make a few minor changes. Thus, it is easier to create the two modules than it is to create PRODUCE HISTOGRAMS.

The two alternatives can also be compared on the basis of flexibility. Consider a possible change. Histograms are to be produced for each office as well as for each broker and for the entire company. PUT HISTOGRAMS has to be expanded to three sets of code, one for each type of histogram. All that needs to be done for the solution in Figure 10.24 is to copy PRODUCE BROKER HISTOGRAM again, make a few simple changes, call it from the top module, and the new report is in place.

Another change could be that the president wants his report to be different. PRODUCE HISTOGRAMS becomes more and more complicated as it keeps track of what to do for each report. With separate top modules for each histogram type, any changes the president wants are simply made to the module which produces his report. For example, he may only want to see certain selected stocks. That can be done by eliminating all other stocks from the quantity matrix before passing it to PUT HISTOGRAM. In all cases, maintenance of PRODUCE HISTOGRAMS requires an understanding of how it produces all three histograms. Separate modules are easier to understand, change, debug, and fix because they can be dealt with independently.

Originally, there was an alternative as to whether to use new masters or broker totals as input to accumulate company totals (see Figure

10.4). Since most people seem to choose broker totals, that was the alternative pursued. But why do most people choose that alternative? Is it not because, given alternatives for accomplishing the same result, it is just ingrained within us to choose the one that has the best performance?

Consider, though, whether the use of new masters as input to accumulate company totals would have led to a quicker solution. The resulting data-flow diagram is shown in Figure 10.28. Assuming the input and output points were picked as in Figure 10.28, the top two levels of the initial chart are as in Figure 10.29. Comparing this to Figure 10.24, this start would have reduced the number of changes necessary to arrive at the final solution.

The Multifunction Specifications

Having designed this multifunction program, it is trivial to design some related single-function programs. One useful program simply updates the master file. What would the top two levels of such a program be like? The top module's name is UPDATE MASTER. The first module on the left is GET NEW MASTER, and there is one output module, PUT NEW MASTER. The structure below GET NEW MASTER would be the same as below the GET NEW MASTER module in Figure 10.24. The same module can even be used. In fact, the whole program can be built very quickly by *deleting* some code out of the module STOCK PROFILE and renaming it UPDATE MASTER (Figure 10.30).

What about a program that produces only broker histograms (from an already updated master file)? Here, the top module's name is PRODUCE BROKER HISTOGRAMS. It simply calls GET MASTER on the left and PRODUCE BROKER HISTOGRAM on the right (Figure 10.31). A program to produce only the company histograms is shown in Figure 10.32. A program to produce company histograms, but from up-to-date data (without physically rewriting the master file) is shown in Figure 10.33. As was indicated earlier, if the designer knows how to design multiple-function programs, then designing single-function programs is just a subset.

Notice the advantages if (in systems design) the functions defined for STOCK PROFILE are each specified for a different program. Three programs would result: UPDATE MASTER FILE, PRODUCE BROKER HISTOGRAMS, and PRODUCE COMPANY HISTO-GRAM (the latter two with or without updating the master file in

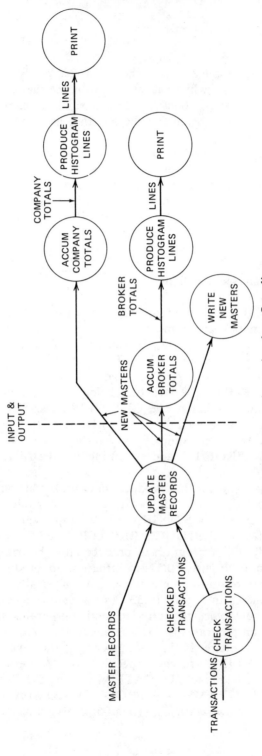

Figure 10.28 Alternative data-flow diagram.

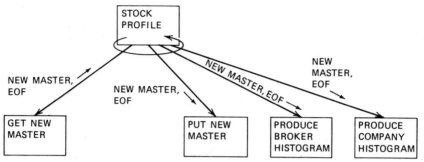

Figure 10.29 Top levels for previous figure.

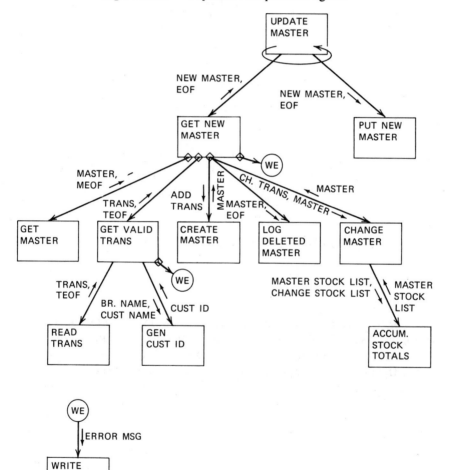

Figure 10.30 UPDATE MASTER.

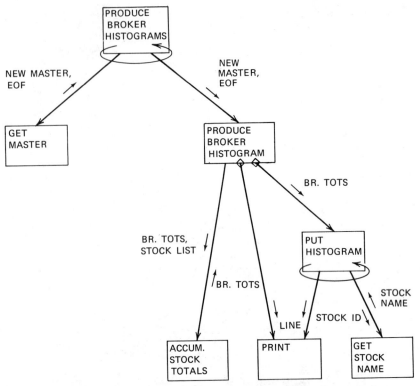

Figure 10.31 PRODUCE BROKER HISTOGRAMS.

memory before printing the histogram). The implementation is easier than with **STOCK PROFILE**, although the difference in complexity is reduced because it is structured. But more important, the company may need the flexibility of running each of these functions separately in the future. In the **STOCK PROFILE** solution, if it is ever necessary to rerun the company histogram, the broker histograms have to be run again too, and the master file has to be updated again, whether or not these functions are needed. Although the functions were (presumably) put together to improve performance (the master file only has to be passed once, rather than three times), this combination could end up *wasting* resources.

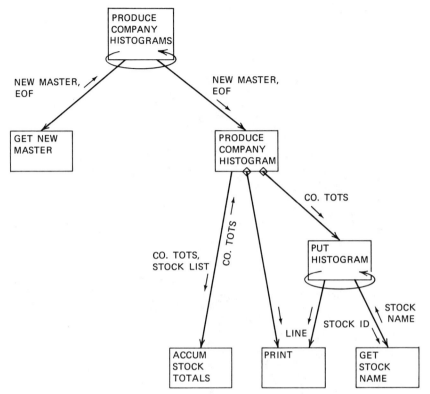

Figure 10.32 PRODUCE COMPANY HISTOGRAMS.

Summary

This chapter takes a set of specifications through a complete design, from the data-flow diagram to a final solution. The specifications were intentionally made simple so that attention could be focused on the design technique rather than on the complexities of a more realistic problem. More complex solutions are modularized using the same concepts and techniques—there are just more design decisions to be made in the course of doing the design.

Once a final structure is derived, reasonable changes are considered from the point of view of how they would impact the structure. As predicted by structured design, reasonable changes are accommodated

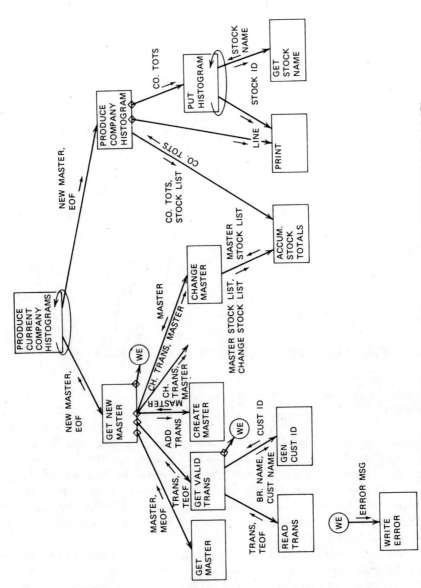

Figure 10.33 'PRODUCE CURRENT COMPANY HISTOGRAMS'.

easily, usually with a relatively simple change to a single module (which can be easily identified)!

The chapter then explores the implications of alternative choices for the data-flow diagram, where there are no rules for choosing alternatives other than that they have to represent correctly the process to be programmed. Two considerations are explored. First, which alternative for the data-flow diagram decreases the time needed to arrive at a final solution? Second, do the resulting two top levels of the structure represent an improvement to the final structure in Figure 10.24, and if not, why not? Each alternative is compared to the solution in Figure 10.24. It is shown how each can be improved into that solution. This is an example of how the final chart is independent of the starting structure, as long as the initial structure solves the specifications correctly.

Finally, the implications of having multiple functions defined for a single program are explored. The structures for programs that each have one of the functions specified for STOCK PROFILE (i.e., UPDATE MASTER FILE, PRODUCE BROKER HISTOGRAMS, and PRODUCE COMPANY HISTOGRAM) are easy to derive from the structure in Figure 10.24. They are simply subsets of that structure (only the top module has to be changed, and that change is trivial). What is more, the single-function programs are more flexible in their ability to provide only the single function *or* any combination of functions required. So as needs change, they provide not only necessary flexibility but possibly better performance, since unnecessary functions do not have to be run in order to run, or rerun, desired ones.

11
Structured Design and Performance

There are two components of performance relative to structured design, execution time and the use of memory. Compiling modules separately has no direct effect on I/O, although the designer has the *option* to dynamically link modules (i.e., read them into memory each time they are executed). But structured design does not require this.

Slightly Better Performance Is Likely

The overhead of a CALL statement in terms of execution time and memory is negligible (as will be explained below). Moreover, there are offsetting performance *advantages* when using structured design that often are bigger than the CALL overhead. Thus, structured design solutions will probably run slightly *faster* and use *less* memory than the typical monolithic solution. By focusing optimization efforts on the critical portions, the performance of the structured solution can probably be made considerably better than a monolithic solution (with the same time spent optimizing).

Execution Time

Use of the CALL statement (as opposed to the PERFORM statement) tends to increase execution time, but other effects tend to decrease it. Execution time tends to decrease because less code has to be executed to handle switches (like those used to keep track of which function is being executed when code is shared by two or more functions). Structured design also tends to result in less complex code, so less code has to be executed in the program.

These effects are small and tend to cancel each other out. In practice, the net result is that the execution time of a structured solution tends to be slightly *less* than for monolithic programs.

While many programmers think that the overhead of a CALL is substantial (especially for COBOL), measurements show it is not. A comparison was done between a CALL statement (to a separately compiled COBOL program, passing *eight* parameters) and a PER-FORM (to a COBOL paragraph). It took 45,000 calls to use one extra *second* of CPU time on a IBM 370/168. Thus, a program which consists of 15 modules, of which an average of 10 are called for each record processed, would have to process 4500 records to accumulate an extra second of CPU time. Processing 4500 records in a program of 15 modules would probably consume a minute or more of CPU time (depending on the program). Thus, the CALL overhead probably adds less than 5 percent to the execution time of a program. Further support-ing that conclusion, timings show that approximately 50 more machine instructions were executed for the CALL statement than for the PER-FORM. Compare this to the machine instructions probably executed for about 50 lines of COBOL source code, including the extra execution of any loops within the module. Note again that this 5 percent is usually more than offset by the items discussed above which tend to decrease the CPU time.

Memory Overhead

It is likely that a structured solution will be more memory-efficient to begin with. Separately compiled modules do require some additional memory for the code that passes the parameters as well as for independent local variables. However, memory is saved because less code has to be included to handle switches, and the code is less complex. The most significant saving, though, comes from eliminating duplicate functions. This results in only one copy of any function ever being in memory. Monolithic programs tend to duplicate functions whenever the target data resides in different records or variables.

For memory-constrained environments, single-function modules provide the maximum flexibility to reduce either overlays or working sets. Only those functions necessary at any one time need be brought into memory. At best, any other physical packaging of modules will have those same functions in memory. It is more likely, however, that the packaging will result in at least some unnecessary functions being brought in with those that are needed.

Virtual Storage

Structured design modules are very compatible with, and probably yield even better performance in, a virtual-storage environment. Execution tends to be localized within a module, using mostly local variables and completing that function before branching to another portion of memory. Early articles on performance in a virtual-storage environment warned against branching out of line, recommending in-line implementation of code when possible. That recommendation, however, accurately applies only to segments of code that are small compared to a virtual-storage page. But structured design modules are much closer to the size of a virtual-storage page than the five- to ten-line segments of code being evaluated relative to in-line versus out-of-line code. Note that if the modules are all exactly one page in size, then "jumping around" is exactly equivalent to executing the next sequential module: one page is brought into memory in either case.

Optimization

Studies indicate that most programs consume 10 to 1000 times more resources in development and maintenance costs than will ever be accumulated in run costs during the life of the program. Thus, for most programs it is not cost-effective to increase the larger development cost in an effort to reduce the run cost, which is already the smallest portion. But for those few programs worth optimizing, the following procedure is suggested. Write the program first in the simple structured format, thus getting it operational as soon as possible. Then, spend all optimizing time on the 20 percent of the modules where 80 percent of the execution is bound to be consumed. This can result in significantly more CPU time saved per hour than optimizing code as it is written, a procedure that spreads optimization time throughout the program and complicates *all* the modules.

The simplest way to gain performance with a negligible increase in complexity is to run the code through an optimizing compiler. If it is necessary to gain additional performance by changing source code, look for ways to achieve the maximum performance while increasing complexity as little as possible. But first get the program running and check to see if it really needs optimizing. Also, fix any problems that arise while the code is still easiest to change. Then consider optimizing, if it is still necessary. A valuable way to optimize code in higher-level languages is to rewrite the module(s) that consume the most CPU time in assembler—and write it the simplest way. While assembler is, admittedly, harder to debug and maintain than higher-level languages, note that the simplest program is already running. The only way to improve the performance is to trade it for some increase in complexity. Writing a few assembler modules in a straightforward manner can cause a small increase in complexity while achieving what can be a dramatic improvement in the performance of those modules. If the performance still is not adequate, take some of those assembler modules and optimize the code.

In all cases, the biggest advantage for the time spent will probably be achieved by restricting the optimization efforts (and increase of complexity) to as few modules as possible—the ones that consume the bulk of the execution time. Using these approaches, it is very likely that, with the same amount of optimization time applied to a program, the structured design solution of separately compiled modules will run faster than a monolithic one.

The time and cost of execution are probably both at their maximum for a program that has just been completed. Technology will see to it that both the execution time and the cost of execution will drop. On the other hand, the complexity of the program is probably at its *minimum* just after it has been produced. Typically the complexity will only grow from that point on. Very few modifications tend to reduce the complexity once the program is implemented, other than rewriting it. Thus, when developing a program it is important not to increase complexity in an effort to gain performance unless it is absolutely necessary. Performance problems will be reduced automatically by technological advances, but added complexity will only get worse.

Separately Compiled Modules

The major advantages of structured design come from the independence and reusability of the modules. The independence is an implemented and assured independence, not just a theoretical, designed independence, which is then compromised by compiling the resulting modules into the same program. Structured designed modules can be tested separately, independent of the rest of the program. Structured designed modules are replaceable: new or improved implementations of the same function can be linked into place without concern for the compatibility of parameter names within the module with those in the rest of the program. Structured-designed modules can be modified without affecting the rest of the program, unless the parameters leaving the module are incorrect or the module calls another module incorrectly (i.e., it still has an error). A modification cannot inadvertently cause an error in other code by, for example, using a local variable that is also used by another part of the program. Structured-designed modules can be reused in future programs simply by being called. These advantages are the point of doing structured design; they are lost if modules are not separately compiled.

These advantages still apply when structured design is used in other areas such as in the design of catalogued procedures, hardware or microcoded instructions, subroutine library functions, functions within nodes of distributed processing systems, and macros. The resulting modules in each of these environments are reusable and do not share local variables (except for macros, which usually use strange variable names to avoid duplicating names already used within the enclosing program). But the only way to achieve these characteristics with assembler and higher-level languages is to compile the modules separately.

For PL/1, using internal procedures as modules is not a viable (performance) alternative to separately compiled programs, since internal procedures *can* still reference all of the variables in the enclosing procedure. Thus the modules will not be as independent as they would be if they were separately compiled. Moreover, performance measurements on at least one PL/1 compiler showed that calls to internal procedures were slightly *slower* than calls to external procedures. Substantial performance can be gained in PL/1 calls, though, by declaring the parameters as static variables. The normal default is dynamic, in other words, the parameters are dynamically allocated each time the module is executed. While this is required if the program must be re-entrant, it is not otherwise necessary for achieving the benefits of structured design.

The major goal of structured design is the independence of the pieces, which is, in part, achieved through functionality. The advantages are not obtained through functional placement of code *within* a program. Moreover, if the modules are not going to be separately compiled, usually much less care will be taken to reduce the number of "parameters" (i.e., shared data elements). The resulting modules become less than really functional, and not nearly as independent as they would be if they were going to be compiled separately. The results of merely placing code in a functional way within the same physical program may not be worth the effort.

Summary

Structured design solutions consisting of separately compiled modules that are statically linked together are probably slightly more efficient than monolithic programs, even without optimization. This is because the overhead of a call is minor compared to the execution time of a typical module. Moreover, that overhead is usually more than offset by the less complex code and by not having to set and interpret switches passed between functions. If optimization efforts are justified, structured design solutions can undoubtedly be optimized to run faster than monolithic solutions, since the optimization time can be applied to the critical areas.

Structured solutions are probably more efficient in terms of memory than monolithic solutions, owing to the elimination of duplicate functions. Moreover, single-function modules provide maximum flexibility for reducing overlays for static storage or working sets for virtual storage. Structured-designed modules are also compatible with virtual-storage environments because execution and data references tend to be localized within one module at a time.

Most programs cost more to develop and maintain than their total lifetime run cost. Consequently, it is counterproductive to spend time optimizing any but a few programs. For those where optimization is justified, look for ways to get the most performance for the smallest increase in complexity. Some optimization techniques possessing that characteristic, ordered by benefit per hour spent, are the following: an optimizing compiler; writing the module(s) with the worst performance in unoptimized assembler code; and optimizing that assembler code (only if forced to). When deciding whether to trade an increase in complexity for a performance gain, consider the following: Execution time/cost of a program will probably get better and better anyway after the program has been produced, owing to continuing improvements in hardware technology. Complexity, however, will probably only get worse.

Using structured design concepts simply to place code within modules that are then physically compiled together will forfeit most of the benefits of structured design. It is difficult to aggressively reduce the number of shared data elements when all the variables are going to be available in working storage anyway. It is difficult to test and change the modules independently. Errors found probably require consideration of code outside of the function. This is because there is no guarantee that other modules can not inadvertently change local variables within the module encountering the problem. Most important, the advantages of reusable code are lost because it is impractical to reuse even functional paragraphs in new programs.

12
Expanded Use of Structured Design

Several considerations are worth noting in an environment where structured design is widely used. They include how to handle the resulting libraries of modules; using structured design concepts for other than the design of a program; and facilities which could enhance the use of structured design.

Module Libraries

A major benefit of structured design is that it can generate libraries of single-function separately compiled modules, which can be used in later programs. It may be questioned whether the complexity involved in managing such a library is worth it. It is, as the following illustrates. First, structured design is justified whether or not efforts are made to make these resulting modules available for future programs. The source and object modules will be kept up to date through the normal maintenance of the programs for which they were written. Similarly, the effort involved in coordinating the changes to a module when it is called by several different programs is independently justified. This justification comes from avoiding having to maintain multiple different versions of the same function, as well as from the advantages of having consistency between functions across programs within the company. Thus, the choice of whether or not to make modules available for future programs is based simply on the effort and cost of providing and using a system to search for existing modules.

For small numbers of modules in a library, a simple search system should suffice. The small amount of time necessary to search for a module even manually could easily be justified on the basis of the development time saved when a module is found. Certainly, no one would consider it advantageous *not* to add modules to the library. Modules are added simply by puting a module description (and location) in a search system. Adding modules increases the benefits, even if the search system remains manual. At some point mechanized approaches to aid in the search for modules will probably be justified by the reduction in time necessary to search for existing modules. Although the complexity of searching increases, so do the chances of finding a module.

Source modules as well as object modules should be available in the module library. Source modules are of course required in order to maintain the original programs, but they can also be very useful as prototypes for new modules. Functions may be needed that are slightly different from those implemented in an existing module. If a new similar module is created which is then modified slightly, maintenance will be much easier than if the existing module is modified to encompass both functions. This process assumes the developer has access to the source of the original module. For example, the top modules of many structures are very similar. Why start from scratch each time when a module with a similar kind of logic is already available? Possibly only a few names need to be changed (as well as the module name) in order to create the top module for a new program. Also, many reports have the same structure. The modules in one can make excellent prototypes for generating modules for structures which implement other similar reports.

Information about modules in search systems should probably include the name and the expanded phrase that describe the function of the module, as well as the module prologue, which gives a more detailed description of what the module does and how to use it. For small module libraries, a hard-copy listing of the module names and expanded phrase, with a pointer to the prologue (in another portion of the document) may suffice. For slightly larger libraries, these items can be put in a simple text file. A text-processing system with a "locate" function can be used to aid in searching.

For large libraries, a more sophisticated searching mechanism is probably justified. Such a system should have the ability to identify which of its entries contains a given word, words, or a sequential combination of words. It should also have the ability to search for synonyms of words and for all words starting with a given set of characters. Library search systems with these capabilities are available. Given this kind of capability, searching for the presence of desired keywords in the prologue may be the most valuable way to find a module, rather than trying to find it by a presumed name.

When changes are made to a module, it needs to be relinked into any programs that use it. As the number of programs using a given module increases, it becomes valuable to mechanize a procedure for keeping track of which programs call each module. A data dictionary can be used to produce the necessary information. If the structure charts are put in the data dictionary, the necessary information can be gained via a "where used" function. If the files accessed by each module are kept in the data dictionary as well, then the "where used" function can also report what modules/programs access each *file.*

It may be desirable to keep modules in individual project libraries rather than in one common library. This reduces the possibility of being prevented from using a name because it has already been used for a previous (but different) module. Detecting and avoiding synonyms is easier because they only need to be avoided within each project library. This way, it is also not necessary to give up one or two letters of each program name to identify the project, as is often done to prevent synonyms. The library search system can handle the existence of different modules that have the same name but are in separate project libraries by using the project library name to qualify all module names.

Use During Systems Design

Structured design concepts can be used during systems design to reduce complexity. Single-function programs are easier to design and implement and are more flexible and adaptable than are programs that do multiple things. Programs that do multiple things also can require an inordinate amount of effort to coordinate and run. They tend to use more memory, and use it for longer periods, than do single-function programs. Their elapsed run time is also longer, which increases the need for, and complexity of, doing restarts for the program. Furthermore, sometimes such programs are run only because *one* of the included functions is needed (and the output from the others is discarded). Thus, as needs change, programs that do multiple things can end up *wasting* machine time rather than saving it.

Large systems usually need to be designed by more than one or two designers. If the designers are designing dependent parts of a system, a high degree of communication is required to produce good results. Lack of adequate communication will be reflected directly in a lower-quality design. Structured design concepts can be used to identify relatively *independent* groups of programs. These can be designed by different designers without needing as high a degree of interaction and communication.

To get relatively independent *groups*, group the programs that work on the same data, that are all dependent on the same thing. For example, the programs that input data to a master file, format error reports (for errors found during the input process), and fix data items (that were found to be in error during the input process) are all related. Programs that create, maintain, and report on the content of a particular master file are also highly related. Programs that rearrange, reorganize, archive, and delete items from a master file as well as report the status of items on the file are highly related.

To design any single program of a group like those indicated above, the designer must understand the file or data dealt with by that group of programs. It would be a good idea for the same designer to design that file also. By having responsibility for *all* programs dealing with a given local file, the designer can have a good understanding of all the requirements for that file and can do an adequate design. This is a lot easier than having multiple designers consult on each one's requirements for a local file, as must happen when multiple designers each have some programs that deal with the same local file. Once the designer understands the file for one program, it is easier for him or her to design any of the other programs in that group than it is for someone *else,* since a second designer would first have to spend time to acquire a good understanding of the same file. Groups of highly related programs are usually connected to other groups by streams of data. In fact, the objective is to group programs so they are only connected to other groups by streams of data (or temporary files). This way a tentative interface can be agreed to by the designers. As long as the interface remains constant, the designers can develop their programs independently. Discussions can be limited to the changes that need to be made whenever one of the designers identifies a deficiency in the interface.

Much more interaction is required between designers when the programs are allocated on a basis other than data, such as by verb. The following are examples of programs grouped by verb: programs that edit data, print reports, do on-line inquiries, or file reorganizations. The designer who would, for example, be responsible for all file reorganizations would have to understand all the files, as would the designer who is designing the on-line inquiries, as would the one designing the edit programs. Using that kind of grouping, all the designers need to know a lot about what everybody else is designing. Either much time is spent in discussions, or the design suffers because of the lack of communication.

Structure charts are not very practical for documenting the relationship of *programs* during systems design. Data can flow between modules only if they call each other. This restriction is not true for programs. Programs can send data to any other program, not only to "adjacent" programs on the job stream. Data-flow diagrams (e.g., systems flowcharts) are much more versatile for showing the possible flows of data between programs.

Designing Interfaces and/or Functions

Structured design concepts and techniques are useful anywhere it is important to design good interfaces and/or functions that are highly usable, flexible, and easy to understand. Thus, they can be used to design macros, members of a subroutine library, and computer hardware instructions, and for choosing functions to be microcoded. Current implementations of these already seem to be functional, flexible, and low coupled. However, those responsible for designing such areas may find that structured design helps to formalize and enhance techniques and concepts they may already be using. Structured design may also be a useful way to help new people rapidly achieve the same level of quality as more experienced people.

Catalogued procedures and catalogued execs can also benefit from increased flexibility, usability, elimination of duplicate function, and easier maintenance. But a wider range of people are doing these, resulting in varying levels of quality. Structured design concepts may be especially helpful for those designing catalogued procedures/execs.

Application generators provide a lot of precoded function. They supply exits where user-written routines can be called to do specific tasks (e.g., field edits). This environment encourages the development of small functional modules. Those already doing structured design will probably find that many of the needed modules already exist in their module libraries. Structured design can enhance the ability of those just starting to use program generators by helping to produce the needed modules and to improve the quality of the results.

Distributed processing is a rapidly developing area. Distributed processing systems need simple, well-defined interfaces between functional nodes, reduced need to pass data between nodes, and the ability to do as much processing as possible at nodes without accessing data from outside the node. These are characteristics and objectives of structured design. Thus, structured design considerations and techniques can be very useful when designing distributed processing systems.

Facilitating Modularity

A number of things can enhance environments where structured design is being used. One is for high-level language compilers to be able to compile multiple modules during the same pass (producing a separately callable object module such that each one has its own distinct set of local variables). Assembler and FORTRAN compilers typically have this capability already.

Another useful aid would be programs that automatically generate structure charts by inspecting object modules and/or the representation of structure charts kept in a data dictionary.

Publications showing structure charts for different kinds of programs would be a valuable way to share the benefit of good structured designs. Even if the charts did not fit the need exactly or could be improved, they would undoubtedly be an excellent start for others who want to design programs which do similar things.

Relative to hardware, implementing a CALL instruction that performs the entire standard linkage convention in hardware or microcode would reduce the overhead which does exist in executing a call.

A routine that traces calls during program execution would be a very valuable debugging aid; just an in-memory trace table would be sufficient. Options to print the table dynamically and/or to trace parameter values would be even more useful.

APL's capability to pass parameters from a caller to a called function is limited. Thus, it is often simplest to define some parameters as global variables. It would be valuable if APL were augmented to include a more flexible parameter-passing mechanism. The following format seems consistent with existing definitions while providing the need flexibility.

FUNCTIONNAME [P1;P2;P3; . . .]

This format would be used both for the call and for the function-header. The parameter names in the function-header would be local variables and would take on the values of the positionally related items in the statement that invokes the function. *Also*, when the function exits, the variables in the calling statement should take on the last value assigned, if any, to the (positionally related) local variables in the function-header. This form for a function-header would be mutually exclusive to the form that accepts parameters on the right and/or left of the function name. This form should still allow the function the option to take on a value, though. A function that returned a value would be indistinguishable from that of a subscripted array to the invoking function.

It would be valuable if environments did not require programming to be nonfunctional or control-coupled. When modules are allowed to be separately compiled, the complexity the programmer has to deal with is reduced. It would be easier if input/output statements to the same file were allowed from different separately compiled modules, and if operating system services could be invoked without the need either to pass control switches or to put and get parameters from control blocks. Complexity would also be reduced if operating systems could always close files automatically when a program exited. Programmers could assign more meaningful names to modules if module names were not limited to eight characters.

Development on small computers and intelligent terminals would also benefit from restricting the range of local variables and from a flexible, versatile mechanism for passing data between modules. A call mechanism suffices, but mechanisms to provide a "fork" (i.e. invoke asynchronously) and/or execution-time data coupling (see below) would also be highly beneficial. Structured design concepts and techniques have been found to be valuable even when writing multiple programs for programmable calculators. Such programs would be even easier to implement if a call mechanism were provided.

The later in the development cycle coupling is established between modules, the more flexible and changeable the program is. Being able to establish data coupling at execution time would yield substantial reductions in complexity and increases in flexibility. A valuable facility would be one allowing the sequence of transform modules for a single data stream to be defined at execution time. Each of the transforms could have one data stream as input and one data stream as output (J.P. Morrison, 1978). A more comprehensive set of facilities could allow not only primary but secondary, tertiary, and so on (as defined by the module) input and output streams to be connected to other modules. Also useful in an execution time protocol would be the ability to direct the same stream of data to multiple modules and to merge or concatenate multiple data streams.

Summary

As subroutine libraries grow, the complexity of keeping track of, and searching for, modules that do needed functions also increases. For medium-sized module libraries, text-processing systems that include a "locate" capability can be used. For larger module libraries, library search systems can be used to look for entries containing given words or combinations of words.

When modules are fixed or changed, it is advantageous to relink the new module into every program that uses it. It is useful to keep the structures in data dictionaries in order to answer "where used" questions regarding the elements within the structure.

It is desirable to keep modules in project libraries rather than in one common library. This reduces the chance of synonyms, and eliminates the need to give up one or two characters of each module name to identify the project.

It is valuable to take structured design concepts into consideration during systems design. Defining programs to accomplish only single functions makes them more flexible, easier to use, and more maintainable. Programs that do multiple functions can also be complex to run and may even *waste* computer time, rather than save it.

Structured design can also be useful for dividing programs within a system into groups that can be designed and developed relatively independent of each other. This greatly improves the ability of a team of designers to work on the same system (when the system is large).

Structured design concepts and techniques are useful wherever flexible, usable, well-defined interfaces and/or functions are of value. This includes the design of macros, subroutines for a subroutine library, microcode, and hardware instructions. The flexibility, usability, and maintainability of many of these may be strengthened through consideration of structured design principles.

Application generators provide exits for linking to user-written modules. Structured design concepts may facilitate the generation of such modules. Designers already using structured design may find that many of the necessary modules are already available in their module libraries.

Distributed processing systems may benefit from characteristics provided by structured design. These include well-defined, simple interfaces between functional nodes; a reduction in the amount of data that must flow through these interfaces; and the ability to do a large amount of processing at functional nodes without accessing data outside the node.

Several things could facilitate the use of structured design, including the ability in all high-level languages to define multiple modules during one pass of the compiler, and the ability to generate structure charts automatically from inspections of object modules and/or from data dictionary representations of structures. Publication of already existing structure charts would benefit everyone. Implementing a CALL instruction in hardware or microcode to perform the standard linkage would reduce the small overhead that does exist with a call. A routine to trace the sequence of calls during execution of a program would be a useful debugging aid.

The ability to pass variables in APL would be enhanced by adding a new form for the call linkage:

FUNCTIONNAME [P1;P2;P3; . . .]

Parameters would be passed positionally, and ending values would be passed back to the caller's parameters positionally. In addition, the function should still be able to take on a value, thus having the same format as a subscripted array.

It would be valuable if all environments, even small computers and intelligent terminals, provided for separate compilations—or equivalent ways to localize parameters and make the modules separately invokable—for example, a CALL statement. Environments furthermore should not require modules to pass control switches or put parameters in control blocks. And it would be easier for programmers to define meaningful names if they could be longer than eight characters.

A very valuable facility would be the capability to pass data to another module without directly controlling when the other module executes, as the CALL statement does. Ideally, the data paths could be specified at execution time. A single data path would be very advantageous. The ability to connect secondary, tertiary . . . etc. data streams would be even more flexible. The capabilities to intersperse and/or concatonate data streams would provide further capability and flexibility.

13

In Conclusion

Structured design makes it less costly to develop a program. But the advantages of maintainability and reusability may be even more significant.

The structured design process is, for programs, similar to designing an office. When an office is designed, functions that are necessary for the office to run are defined. Consider, for example, an office that processes orders. Necessary functions include mailing and internal mail delivery, secretarial support, order processing, back-order processing, delinquent account processing, credit management, and an overall office management, among other things. Each of these functions is specified and staffed. All the necessary movements of data and forms (i.e., interfaces) are specified. Some examples of interfaces are the distribution of incoming orders to order processing by the mail room; sending orders for delinquent accounts to delinquent account control before being processed; referral of back-order quantities to back-order control for follow-up; and sending complete orders to the shipping department.

Once all of the functions and interfaces are set up, orders can be processed. The exact route any particular order takes through the office may be quite complicated. But as long as the processes and interfaces necessary to process each possible part of an order have been set up, the order will be processed correctly. No one ever needed to consider *what* the route would be for all possible types of orders while designing the office. However, procedural approaches for designing programs cause the programmer to have to consider the path each different kind of data needs to take. Checking, testing, and debugging tend to need the same approach. But the paths different combinations of data take may be very complex. Thus the programmer often spends a lot of time considering a great deal of complexity that really need never be considered in order to design or implement the program. If program functions and their interfaces are designed first, then no one *ever* needs to consider the possible paths that complex combinations of data need to follow through the program.

Benefits During Implementation

Designing programs as structures of independent, separately compiled modules can significantly reduce the time necessary to develop those programs. It does so by reducing complexity, which otherwise grows exponentially as program size increases. Structured design is an extra valuable step to insert in the development process. It is done just prior to detailed program design (where is it decided *how* to write the program so it does *what* it is required to do). The time it takes to do structured design is more than compensated for in the reduction of time and effort necessary to test and debug the program. Figure 13.1 shows the typical variation in staffing needed during different phases of a development project. The most desirable situation is presumably to have the curve drop close to zero immediately after implementation. On the basis of the shape of the curve, the chances of this happening are close to

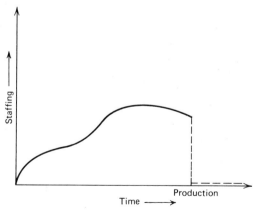

Figure 13.1 Project life cycle.

zero. A curve that is more likely to approach zero at implementation time is shown in Figure 13.2. There will be more effort during the earlier phases of the development effort. Thus, the modest increase in effort during the design phase resulting from using structured design should come neither as a surprise, nor should it be of any great concern. The structured design phase should only continue as long as the simplifications made by the designer are expected to save more effort during testing and debugging than is used by the designer to make these changes.

Benefits During Maintenance

Structured design achieves its benefits by facilitating changes—both for implementing new requirements and for fixing an error. Thus, the same effects that decrease development time also decrease maintenance. One major result of module independence is a reduction of the "ripple" effect. The ripple effect is like throwing a rock into a pool of water. The ripples eventually disturb everything in the pool. There is a tendency in monolithic programs for this kind of effect to take place whenever a change is made. All too often a change causes a new error, which necessitates a new change, which may result in an additional error. When programs get to the point where, on the average, one or more errors result from each change, then the programs are unmaintainable and have to be rewritten.

When the modules are separately compiled and pass only a few data parameters, the *only* way a change to a module can affect any of the

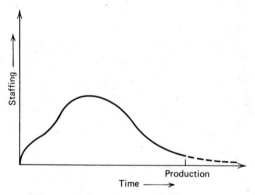

Figure 13.2   A more likely curve.

rest of the program is via the data it shares with other modules. If, however, the module does its function correctly—and this can be tested independent of the rest of the program—it shares only valid data with the rest of the program. If other modules in the program do not properly respond to valid data, then an already present error may be identified in other modules. Using structured design, it is virtually impossible for changes to one module to generate *new* errors in other parts of the program, although this often happens in monolithic programs. Separate compilations of modules are required in order to assure this benefit. Any time taken to "physically package" different modules within the same compile results in *extra* time being spent in an activity that *reduces* the benefit achieved by the structured design effort.

The reduction in staff needed to maintain programs that are modularized using structured design would alone probably justify its use, even if it cost *more* to develop programs using this technique. When it takes *less* time to develop programs that are easier to maintain, then the reasons to use structured design seem compelling.

Benefits for Future Programs

The most important advantage in using structured design is probably neither of the two advantages discussed above (reducing development time for *that* program, and reducing maintenance), but rather, that structured design produces single-function, callable modules. If anything can be used in a future program, a single function can, whereas any *combination* of functions is less likely to be usable. (Note that this reusability benefit is lost if the modules are not separately compiled.)

Programming a computer is hard enough to do. It is tragic to spend time instructing the computer how to do things that have previously been written within the same or other programs. This is especially true when considering that any necessary maintenance must be done separately to each of the implementations. For too long programming has been like creating a painting: the programmer starts with a blank canvas and creates an entire picture. If the computer industry is to keep up with the demand for more programs, programs which are becoming justified by the dramatically decreasing cost of hardware, then it is imperative that the approach be more scientific: Any previous discoveries or developments are made use of, so that efforts can be concentrated on new areas.

There is no development technique which enables a person to write and debug code faster than taking an already existing piece of code "off the shelf." Thus, when one considers future programs, the technique of structured design may be of more value than all the improved programming techniques put together. The advantage of producing reusable code is probably the most significant reason for using structured design. Its value alone would probably justify using structured design, even if it cost more to develop and maintain programs using structured design. But it costs *less* to develop *and* less to maintain programs developed in a way which produces reusable code!

Bibliography

Alexander, Christopher. *Notes on the Synthesis of Form.* Cambridge, Mass: Harvard University Press, 1971.

Myers, Glenford J. *Composite/Structured Design.* New York: Van Nostrand Reinhold, 1978.

Parnas, D. L. "On the Criteria to Be Used in Decomposing Systems into Modules." *Communications of the ACM,* (Association of Computing Machinery), **15,** 12, 1053–1058 (1972).

Morrison, J.P., "Data Stream Linkage Mechanism," IBM Systems Journal, 17, 4, 383-408 (1978).

Stevens, W. P., G. J. Myers, and L. L. Constantine, "Structured Design," *IBM Systems Journal,* **13,** 2, 115–139 (1974).

Yourdon, Edward, and Larry L. Constantine, *Structured Design.* Englewood Cliffs, N. J.: Prentice-Hall, 1979.

Index

APL, 2, 15, 80, 93, 95, 200
Application generators, 199
Array, 49, 103, 201
Assembler, coding in, 2, 85, 105, 192, 200
   connections in, 45, 49, 52, 54
   macro, designing, 1, 2, 192, 199
   as a module, 11, 15, 18
   for optimizing, 191
Asynchronous, 47, 48, 51, 201
ATTACH, 18, 201

Binding, coincidental, 26-28
   communicational, 30-31, 36-37, 123, 137
   definition of, 12, 25
   examples of improving, 101, 123, 137,
      167
   functional, 26, 28, 30-37, 92
   logical, 28-29, 34, 64, 137
   of a module, 36-37
   sequential, 30, 31, 36
   temporal, 29-30, 34, 86
Black-box, 71
Blocksize, 74
Buffer, 109-110

Calls, across levels, 79-82
   number of, 97-98, 167
CALL statement, as linkage, 15, 16,
   57
   in microcode, 200

vs. PERFORM statement, 12, 48,
   188-189
CASE structure, 95
Catalogued procedure, 1, 192, 199
Changeability, as an advantage, 2, 3, 7,
   75-76, 201
   improving, 35, 65, 68, 75, 129, 180
Chief programmer teams, 8
Clarity, 16, 43, 48, 49, 57
COBOL, call overhead in, 189
   code, 1, 11, 41, 110, 176
   connections in, 12, 49, 54, 189
Comments, 19, 86
COMMON, FORTRAN, 49, 52
Communication between designers, 77,
   198-199
Compiles, separate, recommendations
   for, 57, 86, 175, 191-193
   use of, 11, 188, 201
Connections, 41-53
   external, 44-47, 49, 51, 105
   size of, 42, 48-53
Connector, 20
Control, 18, 53-57, 90, 167, 201
Control blocks, 49, 52-53, 103,
   201
Cost, 1, 3, 4, 6, 190
Coupling, control, 53-57, 92, 201
   data, 56-57, 63, 201
   definition of, 12, 40